D1093634

CLARK GABLE

A Personal Portrait

ENGSTED

CLARK GABLE

A Personal Portrait

by Kathleen Gable

Prentice-Hall, Inc. · Englewood Cliffs, New Jersey

LOOK MAGAZINE PHOTOGRAPHS BY EARL THEISEN

Library of Congress Catalog Card Number: 61-14694

Printed in United States of America

T-13508

To my dear husband, Clark Gable,

his friends and fans who love him

ONE night shortly after my husband's death, filled with an overpowering sense of sorrow, I went into his study and knelt beside his favorite chair. I prayed for him and for my dead mother and I wept. Then I felt the soft hands of my young son on my shoulder.

"Mother," Bunker said. "Crying isn't going to bring Pa back but if it helps you, go ahead. In the meantime you're sort of ruining Pa's good leather chair with all that salt."

There will be very little salt on these pages.

I'd like to fill them with the story of the great love I shared with Clark Gable, with the laughter and the immeasurable happiness of our married life, and most important, with what he taught me about dignity, courage, honesty and strength.

Indeed, I needed all of Clark's courage and strength that night I left his hospital room for the last time. They had told me he was gone. But, of course, I tried to hold onto him. Heartstricken, I wouldn't let go. For two hours I held him in my arms.

Finally, I did what my husband would have expected me to do—I faced up to it. Pa was gone. I touched his cold face with my hand, in a last farewell, and I walked out of the room. As I reached the door I told myself I must not look back. I did not.

LOOK MAGAZINE PHOTO

That was Wednesday night, Nov. 16, 1960. I left the Hollywood Presbyterian Hospital crushed by a great grief yet bolstered by a great blessing and an even greater responsibility—Clark's unborn son, the baby he had wanted more than anything in the world.

One hundred and twenty-four days later, in that same hospital, I gave birth to John Clark Gable, a beautiful, healthy child who looks so much like his father that it's almost uncanny. And it's absolutely wonderful.

John Clark arrived on Monday morning, March 20, 1961. I will remember always that it was the first day of spring and that it was one of the happiest and at the same time one of the saddest days of my life.

If only Pa could have lived just 124 days longer. If only he could have held his son just once. If only I could have some sign that somewhere, somehow Clark knows about little John, knows that his boy is everything he wanted.

How many times I have sighed those "ifs" to myself I'm sure any mother can guess. And just as many times I've asked why, why, why? One day, my rugged Little Leaguer, Bunker, came up with a pretty good answer for me.

"Mother, God took Pa because he wanted an extra strong guardian angel for the baby. He can do much more for John in Heaven than he can down here on earth. Besides, one day we'll all be up there with him." The wonderful insight of an 11-year-old.

During those first terrible days I learned something which I suppose many other women have discovered in times of sorrow. If your man loves you and believes in you, you can survive almost anything. Somehow you can do it.

If there is one thing on this earth of which I am absolutely sure, it is that Clark truly loved and believed in me, just as I loved and believed in him. And wherever he is today that still goes.

I remember, shortly after we were married, in one of his rare interviews he made a remark about me. I've always treasured it. He was not one to discuss his family or his personal feelings, but when his questioner brought up my name, Clark boasted, "Old Kathleen has an awful lot of remarkable stuff in her. A lot of good plain horse sense. She can do anything."

So Old Kathleen has done this for Pa. I have carried on just as if he were here. I think this is very important. All of us in this house, his house which he loved so much, have tried to do things just the way he would have wanted them done. Clark was the boss here—he still is. He always will be. Nor will I ever knowingly disobey any of the wishes he had in life.

It is so difficult to go on without him. It was a wonderful life we shared. And I still can't believe it is over. I catch myself waiting for his quick step at the door and his single word: "Ma!" Clark was always telling me how much he depended on me. Now I realize how very much I depended on him—for so many things.

Friends continue to assure me that it will all get easier as time goes by. But I just don't buy that. Understand, I'm not weeping and wailing, because Pa certainly wouldn't buy *that.* What I mean is, deep in my heart it will always be hard for me to be without Clark. I'm not looking for it to be any easier. But I am determined that I will grow stronger and more adjusted. And I'm just as determined to do a good job running Clark's home, rearing his son and his two step-children. We will all have a nice normal life, comforted always by his great love.

I have found comfort from other sources too. The tens of thousands of letters that are stacked in boxes around my little white desk have been a heart-warming revelation of the goodness of people. Of course I have always been aware of my husband's world-wide fame. I knew he had literally millions of fans, and I do not use that word in any patronizing sense. I knew that men and women alike, of all ages and varied environments, admired and respected him.

But although I was aware of all this, still I was truly amazed and deeply touched at the response to his death and the birth of his son. Perhaps because my heart had only been concerned with the private image I was not prepared for the depth of the feelings of those who had loved the public image. Or perhaps in reality the two images were not very far apart.

I say that I was touched by the letters. More than that, the prayers and the understanding so generously tendered by these countless

Army Air Force Captain Clark Gable. I have the identification bracelet he's wearing on his right wrist tucked away for our son, John Clark.

U.S.

Shortly after we met, in 1942, we attended a party at producer Joe Pasternak's home. Here Clark chuckles over a wisecrack of Jimmy Durante's. Frank Sinatra, in white hat, is telling me a story, and Mrs. Pasternak chats with Mrs. Van Heflin. Doesn't my date look handsome in that uniform?

I have always loved our dining room—the fireplace, quaint furnishings, coal oil lamps. This is where Pa and I had our first dinner together.

strangers have made me humble. I mean that. If there was one thing my husband could never stand it was someone who was sincerely insincere.

People sent us gifts; little hand-crocheted booties for John, toys, diaper-pins, beautiful handkerchiefs and even paintings of Clark and the baby done from newspaper photographs. There were also religious medals which had been specially blessed.

At first, as the mail poured in, I tried to answer each letter personally. But even though I enlisted the aid of my sister Elizabeth and Clark's secretary, Mrs. Margareta McIntyre, I soon found I couldn't keep up with the postman. What's more, almost every letter requested a snapshot of the new little Gable or my favorite photo of Clark or some sort of keepsake. Needless to say, I couldn't undertake such a project.

It is my hope that this book will express my gratitude to those who loved and admired my husband and who have been so very kind to me and his new son. In sharing these stories of our life together and these cherished memories of Clark, I may be able to offer some thoughts that will be of help to others who have also lost someone they hold dear.

Of course, there are some secrets Clark and I shared together which are locked in my heart. They will die with me.

As for the pictures in this book, I cannot honestly say they include Clark's favorite portrait of himself. He never had one. In fact, in all the years I knew him I never once saw him express any vain interest in his photographs. He just wasn't that kind of man. You could hand him a batch of the latest publicity stills from the studio and he'd barely glance at them. Admiring Clark Gable, the handsome dream-boy of the screen, was something he just wasn't built to do.

However, I do have a favorite photograph of my husband. You will find it on page 18 of this book. I see it every day, mounted in a plain silver frame, on a table beside our bed. The same picture, in the same type of frame, stands beside John Clark's crib in the nursery.

When I first selected this picture as my favorite I remember that Clark was somewhat amused. "Why, that's an old one," he said. "Look at that old grey pin-striped suit I'm wearing. What do you see in that?"

I saw in that what I have always seen in my husband. I saw honesty and directness. I saw vitality and strength, yet also a gentle kindness and understanding. And, very important, I saw wit, a wonderful droll wit.

Because Clark was such a private person—he was actually extremely shy—there were few who knew the real man. This, then, is the story I have to tell, the story of Clark Gable, the human being.

Clark and I were married for five years and four months. What we had in that time together was so beautiful that at first I felt there were no words to describe it. Then I realized it was really very simple—we had love.

Looking back over that period I wonder if there are many people who even in 25 or 50 years of marriage find the happiness that Clark and I had in those five years and four months. Those who have are truly to be envied.

What does make a marriage work? With us, I think, simplicity was a keynote.

Clark was the kind of man who boiled everything down to the important, basic issues. He was a man who abhorred anything or anyone phony. He had no patience with pretense. He was great enough to be simple.

He loved me and I loved him. Once that was established, we made no bones about it. We didn't play silly games, like trying to make each other jealous. We were too busy trying to make each other happy.

One way we did this was to listen to each other. Pa listened to me and I listened to him. We enjoyed talking together. There was a genuine communication between us. I don't know how the marital experts stand on this, but I think there are too many couples who talk AT each other.

Our enjoyment of our own private gab-fests was the source of both amusement and wonderment to our friends and those who worked for us. I recall hearing our maid Louise talking to a friend a few months after Clark and I were married. Louise, by the way, was my contribution to the household staff. She had worked for me for nearly 10 years before I became Mrs. Gable and I might add she was delighted with my choice of her new boss. She would beam when Clark called her Louisa instead of Louise and, like everyone else on the ranch, she was soon devoted to him. And we were just as devoted to her.

John Clark Gable's father as a baby.

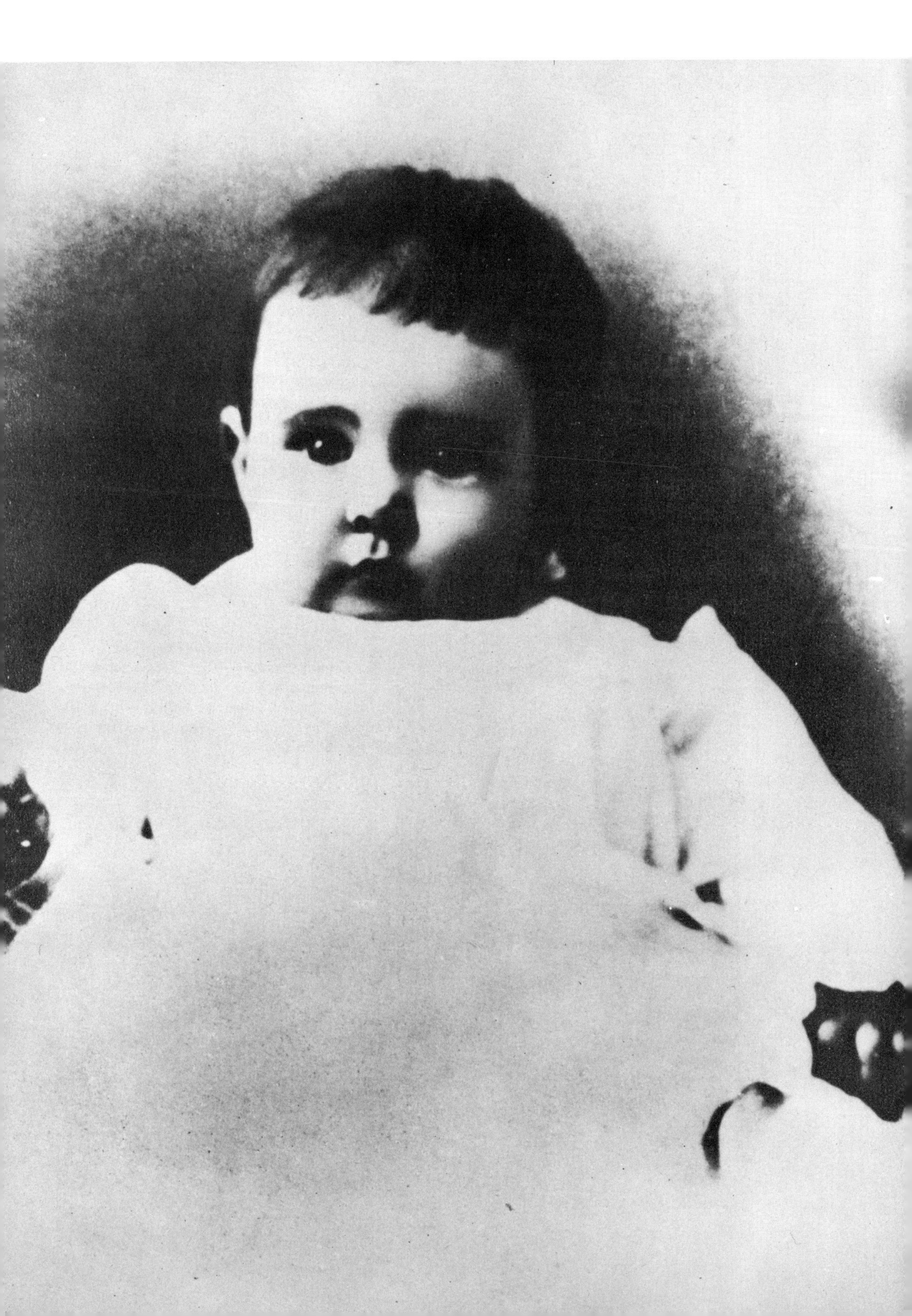

(Above) Clark's celebrated ears were already something to behold when this grammar school photo was taken. But the young gentlemen on either side of him don't seem to be suffering from the competition.

(Left) Clark was about 15 when this high school picture was taken.

But to get back to the story. One day I overheard her talking to a friend. "You just can't believe how happy those two are," Louise was saying. "Why, they sit out there on that porch every night, laughing and talking. Just the two of them, night after night. I hear them and I say to myself, 'don't those folks ever go out?' "

We seldom did. We had our pick of Hollywood's previews, cocktail parties and dinners. But aside from a few parties given by close chums, we turned them all down. I am sure there were many people who felt we were terribly self-centered, snobbish or maybe just plain odd. I don't think we were.

We didn't just sit there on our cozy screened porch and talk about ourselves all the time. Clark loved to read. We also spent a lot of time with the children, Anthony, nicknamed Bunker, and Joan. My previous marriage had brought me two beautiful youngsters for which I will always be grateful. At the time I married Clark, Bunker was five and Joan was four.

Clark was a man of many interests. He had been all over the world. He knew a great deal about hunting, fishing and, believe it or not, gardening. The flowers, the shrubbery, the groves of fruit trees that cover the 22-acres of our Encino ranch home were Pa's special province. He had personally planted almost every tree and he did much of the work around the place.

The vigorous outdoor work not only kept Clark in great physical shape, but he loved it. I'll never forget his delight in the bright red tractor I surprised him with our first Christmas together. Nor his proud grin when he discovered I could handle the thing almost as well as he could. Why not? I used to drive one on my mother's farm in North East, Pennsylvania, 15 miles from Erie, Pa., where I was born.

Now I ask you, does a man who puts in a full day picking his own oranges, repairing fences, romping with two lively step-children, then tops it off with a pleasant, quiet dinner with his wife really need the party circuit? Clark thought not.

But though we loved our beautiful home and spent considerable time there, we weren't exactly hermits. We traveled, went on numerous hunting and fishing trips and played a lot of golf.

CLARENCE S. BULL, MGM

Our dear friend, Minna Wallis, gave this picture to me. She was once Clark's agent. He is shown here, mustacheless, in the first dressing room that he could call his own.

Pa was a good golfer. When we were at our desert home, which adjoins the Bermuda Dunes golf course near Palm Springs, he'd play 36 holes every day. The fact that the thermometer was hitting a hot 116 degrees didn't bother him one bit. Clark had a powerful drive; he could hit a ball 260 yards or more, straight down the fairway. I loved watching him play.

One thing about Pa. Whatever he did, he tried to do it well. He wasn't an impossible perfectionist by any means. But he believed if he were going to tackle a job, he should do it right and give it everything he had. It was this way when he made a movie. In all the years he was a star, he never once was careless about a scene. And it was this way when he played golf.

Clark when he was first under contract to MGM about thirty years ago.

CLARENCE S. BULL, MGM

I remember when he brought home Tommy Armour's book on the subject. It seemed that every time I'd look at him, he had his nose in that book, studying it. He only grinned at me when I kidded, "you must know that thing by heart now." Then, when he'd finally put the book down, he'd spend the rest of the evening practicing his putting in the living room. I had bought him one of those indoor putting greens.

I say that Clark wasn't an impossible perfectionist. By that I mean, while he was never completely satisfied with his performance in a film and always set his goals just a little higher for the next time, he didn't work himself and those around him into a nervous tizzy over it. Pa was

A hair cut on the set for a very young actor.

MGM

John Barrymore and Clark with their skeet shooting pals

a man who was always in complete control of himself. His attitude was, well, I did the best I could. Next time I'll just have to make it a little better.

So even if he wasn't able to out-golf Ben Hogan, he was still nice and easy to live with after a day on the links. Pa and I had some of our happiest times on the golf course. We laughed a lot. He'd play his serious games with his buddies but when we went out there together it was just easy-going fun. Like the time he was getting ready to make a six-inch putt. He made such a nice picture, standing there in the bright sunshine, tanned and trim. Pa wore sports clothes as though they had been invented for him.

Father and son—William Henry Gable, Clark's father, was a most distinguished gentleman. He used to tell me about Clark's boyhood and how much he disapproved of his only son becoming an actor, instead of working in the oil fields with him. Later, he became very pleased with his son's great career in the entertainment world. It was a great loss to Clark when his father died in 1948, at the age of 78. Like Clark, he was stricken with a heart attack.

UPI

He was concentrating so hard, I couldn't resist it. Just as Clark started to putt I said, "Watch America's Sweetheart sink this." The ball went right off the green, smack into a sand trap.

I said before that I thought simplicity played an important part in the happiness of our marriage. I was referring to a simplicity that has nothing to do with money. There may be some who find those two words incompatible. Clark and I did not. It is possible to live very well, yet live simply. Clark and I did both.

Only a fool would argue that it's not pleasant to have all the money one needs. But at the same time, only a fool would believe that the dollar sign is the magic sign that makes a marriage a big success. Clark and I certainly had all the material things we needed. He had worked hard all his life.

I never looked upon him as Clark Gable, the great film hero, not even in the very beginning. I judged him on his own, as a man. Did I like him? Was he my kind of people? That was my yardstick. That's what really counted. I can honestly say I have never been celebrity-conscious. When I first met Pa I think he admired this in me, because he, less than anyone, was Clark Gable conscious.

So meeting a movie star didn't particularly impress me. As a successful model in New York I had tasted the so-called sophisticated life and I met many famous people. I knew my way around the Stork Club, "21," El Morocco and the other high temples where cafe society practiced its gay rites. It was a world of glitter, but I was never completely bedazzled.

Of course I had fun. I was young and I was lucky. At 17, fresh off my mother's peach ranch, I practically fell into a lucrative modeling career. Both my height (5′5″) and my figure were short of the requirements for a top fashion model but it seemed my face went well with the cold cream, breakfast cereal and cigarette ads. By the time I came to Hollywood for a screen test several years later I was earning up to $75 an hour.

I made good in New York, professionally, but I made mistakes, personally. Namely, two brief marriages. Both ventures ended in divorce and I headed for a new life in California.

This was Clark's favorite picture of me. It was taken about the time we first met.

CLARENCE S. BULL, MGM

This is my favorite photograph of my husband. It stands beside our bed, mounted in a simple silver frame. I also have a copy of it on a table beside John Clark's crib so that we are both reminded that Pa's love is always with us. I like the picture because I think it conveys Clark's honesty, vitality, kindness and understanding.

I have read at least three different versions of my first meeting with Clark—all wrong. The most hilarious part of the story, our first dinner together, has never been told.

Actually, I turned down the initial invitation to meet him. It was in 1942, shortly after I arrived in Hollywood. I had a stock contract at MGM, the same studio where Gable was the reigning star.

I was living in a small apartment in Westwood when one day I received a call from Benny Thau, an MGM executive and technically, one of my bosses.

"We're giving a little going away party tomorrow night for Clark Gable—he's leaving for overseas service," Mr. Thau explained. "I'd like to invite you as Clark's dinner partner. It's his last night in town and I know you two will get along well."

The invitation sounded more in the nature of a command performance and I didn't particularly like the idea. Also, I was still upset over my recent marital troubles and I was in no mood for attending a party, the glamorous Mr. Gable notwithstanding.

So I told Mr. Thau I was terribly sorry but I had another engagement which I couldn't break. Shortly after I hung up, the phone rang again. This time it was Eddie Mannix, another MGM executive. He repeated the invitation. Politely, I declined again. Then came a third call. Mr. Thau was back. He thought perhaps I might have changed my mind. I hadn't.

Apparently they just couldn't believe a young unknown contract player named Kathleen Gretchen Williams would turn down a chance for a date with Clark Gable. "I'm sorry," I repeated firmly, "I'll just have to wait and meet him some other time."

That time came about six months later. I remember it was October. The phone rang. This time there were no intermediaries. And there was no mistaking that resonant voice.

"Miss Williams, this is Clark Gable. I'm home on leave," he said. "I'm sorry I didn't get to meet you before I went overseas. I wonder if you'd have dinner with me tomorrow night."

"I'm afraid I'm busy tomorrow night," I answered. This time it was the truth.

"What day *aren't* you busy?" he inquired, sounding just a little amused. I promptly informed him that Wednesday was open and he promptly replied that Wednesday was fine with him. Then he asked me where I'd like to go and I said I had no preference.

"How would you like to have dinner at my house?" Clark asked, adding, "The ranch is really beautiful at this time of the year." I said that sounded lovely.

"I'll scrape up some extra ration stamps for my cook," promised Captain Gable. "I'll call for you at 7:30."

So that was that. Nobody introduced us officially. Clark simply called me on the phone.

That Wednesday night turned out to be an important one in my life. Not because Clark and I instantly fell in love with each other. We didn't. In fact, 13 years elapsed between that first date and the day I finally became Pa's wife. During that time we both got married again. I say the evening was important because it established a warm bond between us—one that was never really broken through all those years though neither of us quite realized this at the time. One thing is sure, that dinner was certainly the most disastrous, yet hilarious meal we ever shared.

The evening started calmly enough. Clark rang my bell at exactly 7:30. I soon learned he rated punctuality as a virtue. I don't think that man was ever late for an appointment in his life.

I can still remember our opening conversation. Clark was in uniform and impeccably groomed. He smiled and I said to myself, "My, he's an attractive man." But out loud I merely said, "Good evening—at last we meet."

He replied, "Yes, but it's been most difficult. You must be a very busy young lady."

Hardly a scintillating beginning, but then neither of us was trying to out-quip Noel Coward.

We headed toward the San Fernando Valley and Clark's Encino ranch. He was right when he said the place was beautiful at that time of the year. Perhaps I'm prejudiced now, but I think it's beautiful at every season.

Clark especially liked this picture of m
and carried a copy of it in his walle

PHYF

CLARENCE S. BULL, MGM

A so-called "glamour" photo of me when I was under contract at MGM.

They used to joke around the studio that Gable's ranch was harder to get into than Fort Knox. It's true that Clark had always valued his privacy and particularly that of his home. The big electric gate which guards the entrance to the property has opened for only a few of his closest friends in the past 23 years. Unlike many of his colleagues, Pa never invited the press into his house or allowed the magazines to shoot pictures.

It wasn't that Clark was a snob or eccentric. It was simply that his innate shyness, his reserve and natural dignity precluded any such wide open door policy.

Naturally, I was curious about the place and I'll never forget my reaction as that forbidding-looking gate opened and we drove the quarter-mile of winding road to the house. It was not just what I saw, it was also what I sensed—an air of peacefulness.

Solid hedges of oleander trees, heavy with their white blossoms, bordered the entire length of the drive. Beyond this, on each side, stretched groves of orange and lemon trees. Their bright fruit did the Chamber of Commerce proud, and indeed it was an impressive sight to a transplanted Easterner.

The crowning touch was the half-mile stretch of Etoile de Hollande climbing roses of which Clark was so proud. He and Carole Lombard had planted them during the early days of their marriage and he always cherished them. So do I.

This picture was taken from a comedy short I made for Pete Smith while at Metro, about the same time I met C. G. I was supposed to be giving my elbows a beauty treatment. Just about this time I decided I didn't want to be an actress, which was fortunate, because I really wasn't very good at acting.

MGM

On this particular evening the blooms certainly lived up to the garden book's description: Very fragrant, very red, very fine. Blending with the aroma of the roses was the fragrance of the night-blooming jasmine. Is it any wonder I promptly fell in love with the place?

The main house, which is constructed of white clapboard and whitewashed stone, had that comfortable look of having belonged there always. The interior was beautifully furnished in an Early American and Provincial style. However, there was nothing gimmicky or too cute about it. Nor did the rooms have that stiff artificial look that too often betrays the hand of a high-powered decorator. They were done in good taste but were not ostentatious, which was a keynote of Clark's character.

The whole effect was one of casual, understated elegance and comfort—a home to be lived in and loved. This was the idea when Clark and Carole first furnished it back in 1939, and to this day I have made very few changes.

That first evening I had no idea that some 13 years hence I would move into that beautiful house to spend the five happiest years of my life. I do recall that I felt instinctively drawn to it the moment I stepped through the door.

Clark showed me into what was then his gun room. He opened a bottle of champagne and served some caviar. We sipped and we talked —the easy conversation of two people getting to know each other. Even then there was no pretense between us. I've often thought part of Clark's great charm was that he never tried to be charming. Nor did I play the clever coquette. I've never been the type, and if I have one strong theory about life, it's that you should always be yourself. If you put on an act, you're bound to get tripped up sooner or later. I've always followed the policy that honesty makes everything so much simpler.

Over the champagne Clark explained that when he entered the service he let his regular household staff go. His long-time houseman, Rufus Martin, a loyal and trusted servant who is still with me today, was working in a defense plant. However, Clark said he could promise me an excellent dinner because while home on leave he had hired a wonderful cook named Jessie.

arole Lombard and Clark when they returned from their honeymoon in 1939.

MGM

Pa with Norma Shearer in *A Free Soul* (1931), one of his first pictures.

About that time Jessie announced dinner. We went into the pine-paneled dining room and I remember noting that despite the enormous size of the room, it appeared quite cozy. Later, I realized that the old coal-oil lamps which Clark always used in the place of candles had something to do with this effect. They cast a warm glow over the area.

Our first course, a salad, was already on the table. But it was the handsome centerpiece which first caught my attention. Two large antique brass bowls, gleaming in the lamplight, were filled with colorful persimmons, pomegranates and fresh green leaves. My host proudly pointed out that the fruit was home-grown.

Hell Divers with the late Wallace Beery.

MGM

I should mention that we weren't entirely alone in the room. Clark had a Siamese cat named Simon, a dachshund named Commission and a beautiful hunting dog named Bobby. The whole troupe had escorted us to our places.

Bobby promptly took up a position by my side, entreating me with his most soulful hound-dog expression. The little dachshund made himself comfortable on the floor beside his master and Simon played the field. The cat, an attention-demanding creature, would brush first against Clark's ankles, then back and forth against mine. I was about to remark that this little act wasn't helping my war-scarce nylons any, when I looked up to see Jessie coming through the swinging door.

She was an enormous woman and she bore a large Spode platter with a tremendous roast of beef, surrounded by Yorkshire pudding and gravy. But what fascinated me was the way she was carrying this splendid feast. That big platter was balanced precariously on one hand, held high over her head in the fashion of a fast-strutting waiter.

Clark told me later that after securing the precious ration coupons for the huge roast, he'd remarked to his new cook, "I don't know this girl and I want to serve her a beautiful dinner. I want you to do everything up in style."

So there was Jessie, toting that platter above her head, her smile a mile wide. I'll never forget that scene. We sat there—dogs, cat and hungry humans—all looking up expectantly, fascinated by Jessie's dramatic entrance.

Then it happened. Just as she approached the table the cook tripped over the braided rug. She went down with a great crash. So did our dinner.

Yorkshire pudding plopped onto the table. Hot gravy splattered over everything, particularly us. And the pièce de résistance, that great, big beautiful roast, landed on the floor along with Jessie. But not for long.

Bobby, a hunter to the core, made the fastest retrieve in history. He also made the fastest get-away. With jaws clamped firmly around the meat, the dog tore out of the room before anyone could recover. Meanwhile, the dachshund was attacking the pieces of beef which had previously been sliced for serving. The cat quickly grabbed a big hunk of

COLUMBIA PICTURES

Mr. G. upset the entire underwear industry in *It Happened One Night*. After seeing this movie, males from Azusa to Zanzibar just refused to wear undershirts.

Another well remembered scene from *It Happened One Night*. I have a 16 millimeter print of this picture, which won Clark an Oscar, and I'm looking forward to showing it to his son as soon as he's old enough.

COLUMBIA PICTURES

MGM

In *After Office Hours* (1935) Clark played a hard-boiled newspaper editor, and Constance Bennett, a socialite society reporter.

MGM

Here Clark poses aboard ship in *Munity on the Bounty,* in which he starred with Charles Laughton and Franchot Tone. Clark played Mr. Christian.

Yorkshire pudding, then fled in terror, literally running up the grandfather clock on the other side of the room. Simon perched up there, his hair standing on end, and unbelievingly surveyed the disaster below.

And Jessie? She was still sprawled on the floor, as shattered as that beautiful Spode platter, crying, "Lawd-eee, Lawd-ee" at the top of her lungs.

Stunned for an instant, my host and I looked at each other. Then Clark broke into a big grin and that did it. We both started laughing and we couldn't stop. We rushed to help Jessie. It took us sometime to get the frightened cook back on her feet. Poor Jessie was no lightweight and throughout the rescue operation she kept moaning "Lawd-ee, Lawd-ee."

By this time Clark and I were practically hysterical with laughter. He had gravy smeared on his face and so did I. My dress, which happened to be one of my best, was soaked through with it.

Clark looked me over. "Well," he said, flashing me that disarming grin, "the first date you have with me, you end up in the gravy. At least you won't forget it. I imagine I've made quite an impression on you."

Jessie, in the meantime, had finally calmed down and Clark summoned his secretary who lived nearby. She drove the cook to the hospital where she was treated for injured pride and a broken wrist. I stepped into a room off the kitchen and slipped into a housecoat.

We cleaned up the mess in the dining room and when we'd finished Clark asked if I could cook. I confessed I was no Escoffier but said I could at least whip up some bacon and eggs, which I promptly did.

So we ended up sitting at the kitchen table, laughing and talking over our simple meal. It was a pleasant ending to a most unusual evening. And Clark was right—I have never forgotten it. How could I—I still have a tiny scar on my knee where a piece of broken china became embedded when I knelt to help poor Jessie.

That first date was followed by many others. We played tennis, golf, went horseback riding and spent pleasant hours out on the water, fishing. We enjoyed quiet dinners at places like Romanoff's and Chasen's, two of Hollywood's favorite and plushiest refreshment stands. And we enjoyed some not-so-quiet evenings dancing at Ciro's and Mocambo and at friends' gay dinner parties. Clark wasn't such a confirmed homebody in those days. I remember one evening he took me to an Air Corps Officers' dinner dance and we had a wonderful time.

I suppose it was only natural that at this time the Hollywood columnists took a great interest in our interest in each other. Everyone understood Clark's grief following Carole Lombard's tragic death and all his friends were hoping he'd find a new life and love. It was inevitable that I should be compared with Carole. A number of the writers pointed out that I bore a striking resemblance to the late actress (which was not true) and had the same gay personality.

Though Clark was also seeing a number of other girls during this period—Virginia Grey and Anita Colby, to name two—still, the Hollywood chroniclers insisted I was the most likely successor to Miss Lombard. They also hinted broadly that I wouldn't have it any other way.

I recall one story which stated I fell madly in love with Clark at first sight and desperately wanted to marry him, but that he was executing a characteristic Gable defensive maneuver. When we stopped seeing each other, about a year after we first met, it was duly reported that I had over-played my hand, had frightened Gable off and as a result was wearing my heart on my sleeve.

I remember that particular cliché because it amused me so at the time I read it. However, the stories and rumors didn't particularly upset me. As a matter of fact, I paid very little attention to them, as I have never nursed much of a desire to see my name in print. Besides, I knew the true story.

It's very simple—Clark and I were not deeply in love that first year. Neither of us was then ready for the strong, beautiful relationship which we were to discover and share some ten years later. Somehow, without ever discussing it, we both sensed this.

To be sure, we were very fond of each other. We were—there's a wonderful Spanish word for it—*simpatico*. We enjoyed a pleasant, warm-spirited companionship. But carefully, we kept the tone light and easy. There was no great, great romance; just gaiety and amusing times together. When we stopped seeing each other, it was without any difficult scenes of parting.

MGM

China Seas featured Clark, Rosalind Russell, C. Aubrey Smith and Jean Harlow.

Clark searches desperately for Jeanette MacDonald after the earthquake in *San Francisco.*

MGM

MGM

In *San Francisco* Clark starred with Jeanette MacDonald and Spencer Tracy. "Spence" was one of the pall-bearers at Clark's funeral. Also shown here is Jack Holt.

In fact, there were no scenes at all. Clark phoned me one night to say goodbye before he left for New York. From there he was going on location for a picture—I've even forgotten the name of it.

Just as we were winding up our pleasant conversation, Clark remarked lightly, "Please, Kathleen, don't get married again." We both laughed, then in the same casual tone I replied, "May I say the same to you, my dear—and bon voyage."

So that was that. Clark didn't write me—not even a scribbled post-card—or telephone me for the next ten years. Nor did I make any attempt to contact him. Why? I suppose a psychologist could come up with a lot of involved explanations, but I believe we were both guided by fate—and fate decreed we needed a little more time.

After our marriage, a close friend commenting on our obvious happiness, remarked, "Isn't it a shame you and Clark weren't married shortly after you first met?"

My answer to that was, "Maybe it is and maybe it isn't."

Clark and Spencer in a boxing scene in *San Francisco*. I remember Pa telling me that the studio hired a professional boxer to work out in the ring with him for technical reasons. Clark and the pro sparred. Results: Clark hit him with his left and down went the pro. He came to an hour later.

MGM

Cafe
Angleterre

You can't relive the past, but I think back in 1942 and 1943, and even for some time after that, Clark had itchy feet. The tragedy of losing Carole Lombard, whom he loved so devotedly, had left him with a deep restlessness. He needed time to repair his own emotional bridges. I think he needed to travel, to be free of responsibilities. Remember, he had worked very hard for years. Then too, there was his wartime service which kept him keyed up and tense.

I, too, needed time to develop and grow. I was 25 when I first met Clark and though I may not have realized it then, I needed time to get to know myself.

No, I don't think either of us was ready for a mature, meaningful marriage at that period in our lives. I've always had the feeling that it wouldn't have worked. But Clark disagreed; a Monday morning Nostradamus, he felt it would have worked magnificently.

Often, during those long happy evenings we spent relaxing on our screened porch, he'd turn to me and say, "Ma, we should have gotten married years ago."

But today, sitting on that porch all alone, I still say, I'm not so sure. True, fate gave us only five years and four months together. But we were ready for them and we used them wisely. With true love and understanding we multiplied those days into the equal of 50 years' worth of happiness. At least I have that to be grateful for.

In the ten busy years that Clark and I went our separate ways we each had our troubles and our triumphs. After being discharged from the Air Corps as a major he returned to MGM. With his wartime service Clark had earned not only the respect of his Hollywood colleagues, but of the entire country as well. Instead of seeking a commission and a soft, Stateside assignment, he enlisted as a private and earned his rank the hard way.

Many of the wonderful letters I have received since his death came from men who trained with him at the Officers' Candidate School in Miami. It was a grueling three-month course, and as with everything else he attempted, Clark gave it everything he had.

Not long ago I was looking through a scrap book a fan had sent Clark and I came across a clipping which made me very proud. It was

Just what he always wanted—an outfit like this. I bet!

MGM

a story which had been filed from an American bomber base in England during the war. A reporter had asked one of the pilots how he liked having Gable, the famous movie star, on the team.

"Clark came here to do a good job and he did it," the flier replied. "He always was a good soldier, never imposed his popularity and took the bad with the good without complaining. He went on some tough missions with us and proved himself a great guy."

After the war the studio welcomed Pa back home with open arms, but the wrong kind of scripts. Clark and the MGM brass started having troubles and couldn't agree on the type of roles he should play. He later told me he knew the films he was given during that period were not right for him and that after a number of bad ones he even began to feel that his career as an actor might be over.

While Clark was having his professional problems, I was busy handling my own troubles. I had long since discovered I didn't particularly like acting and really had no burning desire for a film career. This was fortunate, because it turned out that while I may have been a smash hit in the cold cream ads, I simply couldn't act.

At first I worked hard at the diction, dancing and singing lessons the studio ordered, but after playing a number of bit parts, I turned in my grease paint. I decided to be honest with myself—this wasn't the life for me. Even if I had been more talented, I don't think the struggle and the clawing so often required for recognition would have been worth it.

No, I didn't want to be in movies, but I did want to be in the California sunshine. From the very start I was crazy about the climate. (Nobody had heard of smog then.) Soon after arriving in Hollywood I sent for my mother, sister and brother. We settled down in a house in the Cheviot Hills section and promptly became adopted natives.

My mother was a remarkable woman. Life was not always easy for her, yet she faced it with great spirit. When my brother Vince and I were in our early teens and my baby sister Elizabeth was but a year old, my father apparently decided he'd had enough of farm life. He just took off, and we never saw him again.

It was difficult rearing three children alone, running the farm and trying to make ends meet; particularly when poor weather resulted in

MGM

My husband loved to waltz. Here he is with Joan Crawford in *Love on the Run.*

poor crops. We all worked hard in our orchards—I'm handy at picking peaches, apples, cherries and Concord grapes. Mother worked hardest of all. She was determined that her youngsters would have a good education and she really had to scratch and figure during those rough years.

Somehow she managed. She sent me to St. Benedict's Academy, my brother to Riverside Military School and my sister to Villa Maria Academy. We were always a close family and mother's death of a heart attack in 1953 when she was only 58 was a great blow. It was some comfort to know that we had been able to make things easier for her in her later years. I've often thought that you never truly appreciate the selfless devotion of a parent until you grow up and have children yourself.

How often I've wished my mother could have lived to see my happy marriage to Clark. They had met during the early days of our friendship and she became very fond of him, and he of her. These past years he frequently went with me to put fresh flowers on her grave, just as I often accompanied him to Forest Lawn where Carole Lombard and his father are entombed.

When Clark and I first started dating it always amused him that my mother was so strict with me. Though I was going on 26 and had been married twice, she still refused to give me my own house key. Mother was positively adamant on the subject.

"I may be old-fashioned," she would say. "But I'm still your mother and as long as you live in my house I'm going to know what time you get home at night. So you get no key—you just ring the bell."

In the starring role of *Parnell,* Clark played the spell-binding Irish politician.

MGM

MGM

Myrna Loy, as Katie O'Shea, greets the ailing Parnell as he arrives at her home. (*Parnell,* 1937).

MGM

Saratoga, 1937. Clark with the late Jean Harlow. The rudeness of death so quickly took Miss Harlow toward the end of the filming of this picture. Clark had great respect for this actress and her death added another sadness to his life.

And ring it we did. Clark would bring me home at 2 a.m. after some big party and stand there grinning while mother let me in.

Years later, the day after he brought me home to the ranch as his wife, Clark handed me a tiny, beautifully wrapped box. "Your first present," he said.

It was a gold door key. We both laughed, remembering. I know mother would have laughed too.

Neither Clark nor I took the joking advice we so cheerfully gave each other during that last phone conversation—"don't get married again." Late in 1945, I married again. It was not a happy union, but for the sake of our two children, Bunker and Joan, we tried to make it work. After eight years, I sued for divorce.

Clark's marital venture, while not as lengthy as mine, was equally unsuccessful. His marriage to Sylvia Ashley in December of 1949 ended in divorce 17 months later.

I remember going to a large Hollywood party one evening when I was still married. Clark was there with his new bride. We nodded to each other, introduced our respective mates, then moved on. That was all, and it was one of the few times we glimpsed each other.

After my divorce I sold our large Bel-Air home, and bought a smaller one in Beverly Hills and devoted my time and energies to an ambitious re-modeling job. I had two active youngsters to look after, a house all torn apart and a firm resolve to live alone and like it. The last thing on my mind was a new romance or marriage.

In fact, I had my future all planned. I was going to keep the Beverly Hills house until the children were old enough to go away to school, then I would sell it and move into a nice apartment. Looking back, I don't recall even thinking about finding happiness—all I asked or sought was an absence of turmoil.

Meanwhile, Clark was involved with his own problems and projects and our paths still gave no hint of crossing again. He went to Africa to film *Mogambo,* then to Europe where he played and relaxed a little. He stayed on there to make his last picture for MGM, which was titled *Betrayed.*

UPI

Clark saw great, great talent in these youngsters—Shirley Temple, Mickey Rooney, and Judy Garland—and how right he was! At this time a song was written for Clark called "Dear Mr. Gable." Judy sang it thousands of times. Mr. G. was quite flattered.

MGM

Clark, Myrna Loy, Walter Pidgeon and Leo Carrillo in an anxious moment with an African native in *Too Hot To Handle*.

He returned to Encino determined to get another divorce—this one from the studio. After 24 years under contract, Clark and MGM called it quits. It was no secret around Hollywood that he had long been unhappy with the poor pictures his bosses had given him after the war. He finally decided to break away from the past and make a fresh start freelancing. He wanted the freedom to make his own film decisions.

It was about then that a telephone call brought Clark Gable back into my life—this time for good. I don't know what prompted him to dial my number that rainy afternoon in 1954. To be honest, I never asked him. Perhaps he had been struggling with more than just professional problems. Perhaps he was also struggling against loneliness.

When I answered that phone it seemed as if ten years suddenly disappeared. There was no mistaking that voice. It was just like the first call, except Clark addressed me as Kathleen instead of Miss Williams.

"Would you like to have dinner with me?" he asked casually.

Just as lightly I replied, "I don't know about dining with you—perhaps I should warn you I've developed a rather large appetite. Maybe you'd find it cheaper to send me the money than take me to dinner. Remember, the first time, you had hospital bills for the cook, rugs to be cleaned and I ended up with china in my knee."

Clark laughed along with me, then said, "Well, old girl, I'll take a chance if you will. What night shall we make it? I know you must have a busy social life—any night will be agreeable with me."

So there it was, all light and breezy, just as it had been a decade earlier. We made the date and Clark arrived at my house right on time —as punctual as ever. Joan and Bunker, who were then three and four years old, were on hand to greet him. I must admit I was proud of them. They were all tidied up and earnestly minding their manners, yet full of that natural enthusiasm peculiar to happy four-year olds.

It was Clark's first meeting with the children and they got along just fine. Did I sense, as I watched Bunker solemnly offer Clark his little hand, that these two were soon to be devoted pals, and that we would all be together as a happy family? Hardly.

But I did sense a certain affinity between Clark and myself—that old easy bond of friendship was still there. It was a pleasant evening. We went to dinner and we talked and laughed and the waiter didn't drop the roast beef. Or did we order steak?

Yes, it was like old times and still it was different. Clark had changed and I had changed. It would be strange if we hadn't. We'd both been matured by trouble and time, yet I don't think we were really embittered or soured. We didn't get into any profound discussions that night, but one thing was tacitly understood. At 36 and 53 we were equally determined not to make any more mistakes.

As we said goodnight, Clark casually asked, "What's on your schedule for tomorrow?"

"You are—if you care to be," I replied. I saw no reason to be coy. It had been a nice evening and we had both enjoyed being together again.

So Clark was on my schedule the next day, and the day after that and the day after that. In fact, with the exception of the periods when he was away on location, we saw each other every single day for the next year.

After a few months, I think we were both aware that under our gentle cultivation, the old friendship had blossomed into a truly beautiful courtship. It was a wonderful, harmonious year, a fitting prelude to (the great music of our lives)—our marriage.

While Pa and I shared the same laughter and gaiety which had marked our first relationship, this time the excitement and fun were based on a solid foundation. This time we also shared understanding and compassion. At long last, we were deeply in love.

We had such a good time that year. Though we didn't do anything very pretentious, it all seemed exciting and marvelous to us. We went on picnics and we played golf and we enjoyed quiet little dinners which I would prepare and serve by candlelight. We also spent considerable time with Bunker and Joan. Clark relished the new experience of having youngsters about and they quickly returned his affection. They loved visiting his ranch, helping us pick oranges and just romping about the place. But the main fascination was a gentle burro named Baba. The mule was a gift to Clark from Grace Kelly, whom we both admired. The children spent many hours trying to stay astride Baba, and just as many falling off. But their pal Clark was always around to make sure they didn't get hurt.

Pa got a big kick out of reading to my little pixies, as he so often called them. The minute he'd arrive in the evening they'd rush for their story books. At this time Clark was filming *Soldier of Fortune* at Fox and he'd hurry over from the set without even stopping to remove his makeup.

"I just couldn't wait to get here," he'd say, as we greeted each other. Then I'd fix his one before-dinner cocktail and he'd settle down in a comfortable chair and read the children their bedtime story.

Watching this little scene one evening, I couldn't help smiling to myself, thinking of a remark that had been repeated to me earlier that day. A famous and glamorous actress who had dated Clark in the past was discussing our renewed friendship.

"He'll never marry Kay," she insisted. "Clark doesn't like children—those two of hers will scare him off."

How little she knew. In fact, how little anyone knew. Though by now the movie columnists had duly noted our dates and had speculated about the romance, I think almost everyone privately agreed with the actress. When asked about marriage, Clark and I both gave the same answer—we had no plans.

We really didn't have any such plans until just before Clark left for location on *The Tall Men* in Durango, Mexico in April of 1955. By this time we both knew we had something wonderful, but we had yet to put anything in words. Often, in discussing some future project, Clark would casually say, "we'll do this," or "we'll do that." But I never once asked him exactly what he meant by that word "we."

The camera catches Clark actually rescuing Myrna Loy from a plane used in *Too Hot To Handle* when the "controlled" fire got out of control.

MGM

MGM

MGM

(Above) Pa and Norma Shearer in *Idiot's Delight.*

(Right) Pater taught me this dance step he learned while making *Idiot's Delight.* In the background, at left, I see my dear chum—Paula Stone.

Then, one lovely spring afternoon Clark and I were sitting beside his pool, idly admiring the nearby roses. I remember he was wearing a sport shirt and slacks and I was dressed in a blouse and skirt.

Clark turned to me. "Kathleen," he said quietly, "don't you think we've known each other long enough—we've really been in love so many years. Don't you think we should get this little job over with and become Mr. and Mrs.?"

For an instant I think I must have stopped breathing. Then I answered, "I really don't know, darling. I'll have to think it over. Will you give me about five seconds?"

He said "Yes" and then I said "Yes."

We smiled at each other. "Now, please propose to me again, darling," I said.

Clark reached for my hand. "Kathleen, will you marry me?"

"Yes," I repeated.

We sat there by the pool for some time, savouring the happiness and contentment that at last was ours. We held hands and talked. Clark wanted to buy me an engagement ring but I insisted I didn't need any jewelry. At one point Clark said, "For nearly a year I've had it in my mind to ask you to marry me, but I waited for just the right time. This was it." I readily agreed it was.

Another thing we both agreed on that night was to keep our wedding plans a secret. In the first place, we couldn't set a definite date or work out any details until Clark returned from location and the picture was completed.

So he went off to Mexico and this time there were plenty of letters and calls. Every night at 8 o'clock my phone would ring and the Mexican long-distance operator would announce, "Hallo, hah-nee, your lov-err, he is calling you." Then my "lov-err" would tell me how much he missed me, how the day's shooting went and how he could use some large cans of red-skinned peanuts and also some cartons of American cigarettes. We'd talk for at least 45 minutes, plenty of pesos worth, much to the delight of our little Latin operator who usually stayed on the line, in case the connection was broken. I think she enjoyed our conversations as much as we did.

When Clark returned home we started planning for the all-important day. We were determined that the ceremony be simple and private—we did not want to exchange marriage vows against a background of flashbulbs. We knew if we applied for a license in California, where the waiting period is three days, the press would most certainly be alerted. A surprise elopement to some out-of-the-way spot in Nevada seemed to be the only answer.

At this point we let two others in on our wonderful secret. Clark called his old friend, Al Menasco, and his wife, Julie, at their ranch near St. Helena in Northern California. Pa explained he needed their help in planning the logistics of Operation Wedding.

Al, a retired automobile dealer, scouted Western Nevada for a likely site. He reported back that the tiny town of Minden, some 45 miles south of Reno, seemed the best choice. The Menascos purchased two simple gold wedding bands for us in San Francisco. Had Clark himself bought the rings from a local jeweler, it would have been a sure tip-off.

Finally all the details were settled. We would drive to Gardnerville, Nevada, where we would meet the Menascos under a certain grove of cottonwood trees at 5 p.m., then proceed to Minden, a few miles away.

The night before, Clark drove me to the home of my sister, Mrs. Elizabeth Nesser. We told her our plans and asked her to be my matron of honor. Liz was delighted; she had always adored Clark. "Well, it's about time," she remarked. "I only wish Mother were here to see it."

Then we called on Howard Strickling, Clark's long-time close friend. As vice-president in charge of publicity at MGM, Howard had often counseled Clark in his relations with the press. Pa knew that once we were married the news was bound to get out and he felt the best way to handle the situation was to have Howard issue a simple, straightforward announcement.

"Kathleen and I are getting married tomorrow," Clark told him. "Al Menasco will phone you after the ceremony, when we're safely away, and then you can tell the reporters."

So at last our wedding day had arrived—July 11, 1955. It was a beautiful morning. The sun was bright and warm, even at 6 a.m. when Elizabeth and Clark and I started out in his new white station wagon.

We were all a little keyed-up and as we headed into the blistering desert temperatures we became a little more so—we had car trouble.

Clark, always punctual, was determined not to be late for our rendezvous with the Menascos. A temperamental new car with a bad oil leak wasn't going to throw HIS wedding day off schedule. So we pulled into a gas station, picked up six cans of oil, and continued on our way. Every hundred miles we'd stop and take turns pouring the oil into the car.

We were rolling along at a pretty good speed when we were startled by what sounded like a small explosion. Clark immediately pulled to the side of the road and in a resigned tone announced, "I think we may have a flat."

This scene must have been a gesture on Clark's part to revive the men's undershirt industry which had suffered such a blow when he appeared undershirtless in *It Happened One Night*. Here he is with Norma Shearer in *Idiot's Delight*.

MGM

MGM

Clark and Hedy Lamarr in *Comrade X*.

We all piled out of the car but were relieved to discover all four tires were fine. As we started off, still pondering the source of the frightening noise, I sniffed a vaguely familiar odor. A quick check of my overnight bag solved the mystery. The high desert temperature had proved too much for the can of hair spray I had tucked in one corner. It had literally blown its top. Luckily nothing else in the bag was damaged, as I had carefully packed everything in plastic traveling cases.

As we approached Gardnerville after the long hot drive we faced one more problem. We wanted to freshen up and change to our wedding outfits but I was apprehensive about stopping at a motel. Clark was always so easily recognized and after all our cloak-and-dagger planning, I didn't want our secret discovered so close to H-hour.

I noticed a thick clump of trees beside a stream a short distance from the road. "Why don't we pull over there—we can change behind the trees and freshen up in the stream?" I suggested.

I'll never forget the look my sister gave me. "I have news for you," Elizabeth said dryly. "I'm not about to wash up for your wedding in a babbling brook like nature girl. We'll go to a motel—I have it all figured out."

So we followed Elizabeth's plan and it worked beautifully. We stopped at a place in Gardnerville and she went into the office and asked for two rooms for an hour or so. "My parents and I are on our way to Lake Tahoe," she explained, "but the warm drive has been so tiring, they need to stop and rest a bit."

My sister and I then carried our luggage to our room and Clark's bag to his. He waited in the car until we signaled him the coast was clear. Then, impersonating Liz's tired old father, he started toward the room. He had put on his dark glasses, pulled his hat down over his face, and humped his shoulders like an old man.

Liz nudged me. "Look out the window at what's coming, Kay. It's not too late to change your mind."

Our secret still safe, we quickly showered and changed. My wedding outfit was a new navy blue Irene suit, cut simply, matching navy pumps, and fresh white gloves. My only jewelry was a necklace of pearls. I wore no hat and, incidentally, no hair spray. There was a particular reason for my choice of the suit. Clark had always liked Irene suits on me and on my wedding day, as on every other day, I dressed to please him.

The groom-to-be, handsome in a dark blue suit, white shirt and simple dark tie, readily confessed to a slight case of jitters. Elizabeth and I had packed a little lunch and she surprised us with a bottle of vodka, suggesting a pre-wedding toast. But Clark refused.

"I'm too nervous to eat and I don't want anything to drink either," he said. "We'll have something after we're married but not a drop of anything now. I want to hear every word of that ceremony."

This tattered trio (Clark, Joan Crawford and Ian Hunter) starred in *Strange Cargo.*

MGM

We left the motel and drove down a pretty little lane to the appointed spot under the cottonwood trees where we met Al and Julie Menasco. Right on time, too, Clark happily noted. Our friends had thoughtfully brought along two little sprays of fresh lily of the valley; one for Clark's lapel and one to pin on my suit.

In Minden we applied for our license. The little grey-haired clerk was quite excited when she saw Clark. We asked her not to tell the press or anyone else until after we had left. She smiled, then bargained, "If you give me an autograph for my daughter, Mr. Gable, I promise not to tell anyone."

We arrived at the home of the Justice of the Peace at five minutes to six. It was a tiny cottage, covered with climbing roses. We entered the living room which had a quaint, old-fashioned air about it. I remember noting an ancient horsehair sofa—the kind one doesn't sit on for very long—and lace curtains and old photographs on the walls. On the far side of the room stood an equally ancient organ.

Judge Walter Fisher, who doubled as the station master at the depot, was an elderly man with sparkling blue eyes. He became quite flustered when he recognized Clark. Finally, pulling himself together, he opened his book and the five of us gathered solemnly before him.

The Judge started to speak, then paused. He looked across the room as if a sudden thought had occurred to him, then he uttered an urgent "Oh!" My sister guessed he had suddenly decided we might want a background of organ music. But no, the Judge had just realized his potato soup was burning. He dashed to the kitchen, turned it off, then returned and started the ceremony.

With moist eyes, I looked at Clark. Happy tears also glistened on his cheeks. The Judge instructed me to put the ring on Clark's finger. His hands were shaking, so were mine and so were the Judge's. I struggled nervously with the gold band, unable to force it over the knuckle. Then I remembered that Clark had injured that knuckle long ago and that we had previously agreed he would wear his ring on his little finger.

At last the Judge pronounced us man and wife. Clark and I turned to each other, unashamed of our happy tears. It was a precious moment —we had waited for it so very long.

MGM

MGM

(Top right) As the famous Rhett Butler. (Top left) Vivien Leigh and Rhett on the riverboat in *Gone With The Wind*.

Here, with the beloved Hattie McDaniel, my dearest husband so tenderly touches and looks at his baby in *Gone With The Wind*. I have the feeling he is looking down upon our son with the same expression.

MGM

MGM

Rhett plays up to the widowed Scarlett as Melanie (Olivia de Havilland) looks on.

Rhett and Scarlett ready to start the waltz.

MGM

We hurried to a nearby airfield where Al had chartered a single-engine plane to fly us to his isolated hilltop home in the Northern California grape country. He and Julie had graciously turned their home over to us—for five days we would have the place all to ourselves.

After exchanging warm goodbyes, we winged off to St. Helena in the Valley of the Moon. I've always thought that such a lovely name. We landed in a vineyard where a car was waiting to drive us to our honeymoon hideaway. The long drive up the mountain was made in comfortable, happy silence. Holding hands and looking out at the fields of grapes so still in the summer twilight, we felt as if we were in another world.

Our tactful driver deposited us at our destination, then quickly departed. For a moment we stood looking at the attractive little rustic house, then we walked across the front porch. Just as Pa opened the screen door, I turned to him and announced dramatically, "Clark Gable, this is your wife!"

When we finally stopped laughing, Clark kissed me and said, "Well, it's about time—and I love you."

Inside the house we found a lovely surprise. On top of a quaint old woodburning cook stove which stood in one corner was a big washtub decorated with ribbons and flowers and filled with iced champagne—the nicest wine cooler I'll ever hope to see. A beautiful wedding cake stood on the long, pine-paneled dining table. The refrigerator held tempting platters of cold roast pheasant, potato salad, dill pickles—all the foods Pa loved.

Fresh bouquets of daisies blossomed throughout the house and there were several bowls of jelly beans and old-fashioned mints, Pa's favorite candies. Our dear, thoughtful friends, the Menascos, certainly hadn't overlooked a thing.

After changing to a white hostess gown (when I selected my trousseau I kept in mind Pa's dislike of ruffles and frills), I arranged our wedding supper on the table. Clark opened a bottle of champagne and carefully filled our glasses. He raised his in a toast. "Mrs. Gable." I raised mine. "Mr. Gable."

Suddenly, the sentiment of the occasion overwhelmed us and for several minutes happy tears diluted our wine. Finally, emotion gave way to hunger and we ate heartily.

When we finished eating, I cleaned up the dishes and we put in a call to the children. They were excited and full of questions. "When are we coming to live with you and Judge Fisher?" they asked. They had heard the news on the radio but had evidently misunderstood.

"I didn't marry Judge Fisher," I explained. "I married Clark Gable."

"Oh, you mean that nice man with the *mus-tack* who reads us stories and has real oranges on his trees?" I assured them I did indeed mean that nice man. We promised we'd be back with them soon and we all said goodnight.

The front entrance of our ranch house. I used to sit on these steps and chat with Clark's father, whom I loved.

MGM

MGM

Our bright, gay living room—exactly the same as it was from the beginning. On the far right you see part of Clark's favorite overstuffed chair—the one Bunker was slowly wrecking.

Mr. G's study upstairs. Our differences were usually settled in this room. I now use it for meditation, and if the children have problems, this is where we straighten them out.

MGM

After five serene days on our mountain top, Clark said, "Kathleen, where would you like to go for your honeymoon? Europe? South America? The Orient?"

"I want to go home—to the ranch," I said, and that is where we went.

As Clark and I approached the front door I thought of my first visit to the ranch nearly 13 years before and how I had instinctively felt drawn to the place. However, this time my entrance was different—my husband carried me over the threshold.

Though he was not overly glib with words, Clark was a man of great tenderness and understanding. His concern for my feelings and his unselfishness always touched me deeply. The day we returned from our honeymoon he turned to me and said, "Kathleen, you don't have to live here if you don't want to. We can sell the ranch and buy a house in Bel Air or Beverly Hills or wherever you choose. It doesn't matter to me—all I want is for you to be happy."

I looked around the comfortable room, still furnished with the pieces Clark and Carole had selected so many years ago. I knew what Pa was thinking, but I felt no jealousy, no rivalry with the past. I was haunted by no ghosts.

I knew Clark loved his home more than any place in the world and I knew I did too. So I smiled at him and said, "No Pa, I want to live right here. We both love the ranch. It's an ideal place to bring up children. Let's not ever think of moving."

From the start, Clark made it clear I could make any changes I wanted in the house. It was my home, to run just as I saw fit. That first day he took me into the kitchen where he had gathered the household help. "Mrs. Gable is in charge of this house now," he announced, pleasantly but firmly. "She'll make all the decisions, and you'll go to her with any problems." He grinned at me as he added, "Her job will be the inside, I'll take care of the outside."

However, I had no desire to re-do Clark's home, change his way of life or influence his film decisions. I didn't marry him to change him, to mother him, or to manage his career. I married him simply to love him.

We settled down to a happy, harmonious life with Bunker and Joan, who soon were referring to that nice man with the *mus-tack* as "Dearest

Stepfather." The children adored Clark and he was devoted to them. But he was careful not to spoil them. It didn't take the youngsters long to learn they couldn't put anything over on him and they quickly respected his position as the head of our house.

Everything I did had just one thought behind it: Pa's happiness and comfort. I keyed my life entirely to his needs. His path was the one I chose. This called for a few adjustments on my part. In the beginning, I didn't really enjoy tramping through some damp field all day, wiggling under barbed wire fences and lugging a gun I wasn't allowed to shoot. (Pa insisted I carry an unloaded gun until I could handle a loaded one safely.) But I believe an important part of marriage for a woman is in doing what her husband wants. If you love him enough you can learn to like what he likes.

So I stocked up on hunting clothes, long warm underwear, slickers and boots, and wherever he went, I went. I learned to shoot and fish and I played golf. And it wasn't long before I discovered I was genuinely interested and loved our trips as much as he did.

It was a wonderful life we shared—there was such harmony between us. In fact, we were so close, Clark used to say to me, "I know what you're thinking before you even say it." And most of the time he did. There wasn't a lot of chatter between us about love. It was so strong it didn't need words. Nor did we need a lot of people around.

We rarely entertained, and we never gave big, elaborate parties. During all the time we were married we gave only two or three dinner parties a year, and then we never invited more than 12 people at a time. We seldom went out ourselves. To put it simply, we'd both been out.

In his 30 years as a public figure Clark had been everywhere and seen everything. Now he longed only for the contentment he found at home. I, too, had had all I wanted of the party circuit, the gay social whirl. Clark and I had a favorite phrase which beautifully summed up our attitude—he used to say, "Ma, we've both been to all those fires."

And so it was that we stayed home and tended our own, and together discovered the wonderful art of doing nothing, and doing it well. One day Clark said, "I want to see what it's like to retire." So he took a whole

These old brick steps at our ranch are saturated wit
sad and happy memories for me. Here we have returne
from our five-day honeymoon at St. Helena, Californi

U

LOOK MAGAZINE PHOTO

(Left) This burro, who answers to the name of Baba, was given to Clark by Grace Kelly, whom we both admired. The children spent a good deal of time trying to ride Baba, and almost as much time falling off him.

(Below) Mr. Green Thumb loved his garden. He planted most of the trees and shrubs at our Encino home more than 20 years ago. I'm helping him cut the beautiful red Etoile de Hollande roses he loved. Lilacs were also one of his favorites. We have one especially lovely bush. Sometimes it shows up with just one bloom because it needs the freezing weather for its full development. I don't have the heart to remove it. If it freezes over some day and blossoms out as it should, I'd like to take a bouquet from it for Clark's grave.

LOOK MAGAZINE PHOTO

year off and we spent every single day of those twelve months together. They went by as fast as you can lift an eyelash and we were never bored with each other.

One afternoon when we were sitting on our screened porch admiring the shape of the new elm Pa had just planted, he remarked, "Kathleen, we do nothing better than any other couple in the world. I hate to go anywhere," he added. "You've made it so comfortable for me here. You and the children have brought me something I've never known before—a real family life. This was a lonely house before—now it's a real home."

For the sake of Clark's son and his two step-children I intend to keep it a real and a happy home. But for me there will always be the difficult hours when once again it is such a very lonely house.

Looking back on our days together I can honestly say there was never any dissension. Neither Clark nor I could stand nagging or quarreling. Of course we had little disagreements now and then. Show me a married couple that doesn't. But these problems were never discussed at meal time or in the presence of the children or others. They were worked out by Clark and me ALONE, until a point was proven and the disagreement settled in favor of one view or the other, never to be mentioned again. And there was no "winner" and no "loser."

These conversations always ended up in an amusing vein, taking any bitterness out of the argument. We'd laugh together at something and it was like the fresh orange-scented breeze which often sweetened our bedroom at night. Then it was off to bed with clear thinking and an hour or so of reading, followed by the goodnight kiss and untroubled sleep.

One of the reasons our marriage was such a success was that we lived in the present, not the past. We never held up past experiences to each other. I know many people have been curious as to my feelings about Carole Lombard. I never met her, never saw her in my life, except in films. But I have always had the greatest respect for what she and Clark had together. I think he knew this and admired it without ever saying it. When you're deeply in love you don't have to put things into words. You know the other one understands.

Carole was a part of Clark's life before I ever met him. Why should I be jealous or resent that? Clark rarely discussed other women or past sweethearts. He just wasn't that kind of a man. Oh, now and then he'd mention some of the silly things he and Carole used to do, but he never made comparisons. Nor did I seek them. I never said, "Did you love Carole better than you do me?" The love he had for her and the love he had for me were never discussed together. We were living in the present and looking forward to the future.

True, we called each other "Ma" and "Pa," just as he and Carole did. But names such as these are natural to any devoted couple. Clark never called me Kay, as so many of my friends do. "I like the full name, Kathleen," he used to say. "It sounds lovely."

Sometimes I'd tease Clark about that word "Ma." "You had so many sweethearts, you couldn't always remember their names," I'd say. "So you called each one 'Ma' and that way you couldn't get into trouble." I'd be rewarded with a big grin.

While we had a simple, casual home life it was never haphazard or disorganized. Clark was a wonderfully neat man, about his person, his wardrobe and his home. He had no patience with disorder or untidiness. He expected his home to be run smoothly and well and I always saw to it that it was.

I believe, in any marriage, regardless of financial status, it is up to the wife to give just a little bit more than the husband. After all, she has more to gain from marriage than he. And so it is her duty to see that everything is kept in as perfect order as possible and that, within reason, the home life is geared to please the husband.

Most important, I feel a woman should handle all the little household problems herself. I made it a rule never to bother Clark with these things. It must be an awful bore for a tired husband to come home and be greeted with a lot of chatter about how badly the children behaved, how the dishrag went down the garbage disposal and how the dog tracked mud on the floor.

I tried to make our home a place of comfort, a haven of serenity. To accomplish these things, a woman must give a little more than the man. But why make marriage a battleground for equal rights for each

Clark dug all of the holes for the fence posts on our ranc[h]
Band-aids for blisters courtesy of Mrs. Gabl[e]

LOOK MAGAZINE PHOT[O]

partner? Does it really matter how each side measures up as long as the sum total is happiness? I thought not. And I am thankful that early in our marriage I discovered pleasing Clark really gave me greater satisfaction than pleasing myself.

Of course, I realize it's far easier to maintain a smooth-running home when you have good household help. But I think any mother will agree that even with ample help, two children and a big house cannot be properly managed with just the left hand. You're not doing a good job if you operate by remote control from the beauty shop, afternoon bridge games or daily shopping expeditions. I gave my husband, home and children my full attention, and I enjoyed every minute of it.

When Clark was working on a picture we had an invariable routine. We'd get up at 5 a.m. Pa was one of the most conscientious actors in the business. He was never late on the set and he always knew his lines.

Pa halts at our stables at Encino before taking off for an early morning ride with Melody.

Pa loved dogs. His favorites, Commission and Bobby, pose with their master. They're the culprits who ate our roast beef dinner when it landed on the floor during our first date.

Each night he'd prepare for the next day, going over his script umpteen times until he was satisfied. Some mornings he'd still be concerned about a particular scene, so while he was dressing I'd sit on the bed and, between yawns, cue him.

Once in a while, when I'd come upon a tense, romantic line, I'd enliven the proceedings with a dramatically corny reading. Pa would stop shaving and fix me with his best scowl. "Please, Kathleen, no emoting. Just read the lines." Then I'd counter with, "Well, if you don't like my style you can always pay your dialogue director to come up here at 5 a.m. and cue you."

But there was one line we always delivered straight to each other, no matter what time we got up. "Good morning, darling—I love you." Or sometimes Pa would smile at me and say, "You know Ma, I'm a very happy man." Need I add that this made me a very happy woman?

Clark always called me during his lunch hour, but I rarely visited the set. I saw no reason why I should go to the studio—if I had been married to a banker I wouldn't have gone to the bank. In fact, I made it a rule never to interfere with Clark's work. He seldom brought home studio problems, and if he did mention something I never offered advice. And I tried not to ask too many questions. Pa was not a man to bring gossip home from the set. In fact he was not a man to gossip at all.

Clark was extremely popular with those who worked with him. He was always considerate and friendly to everyone on the set. He never made temperamental demands, never held up shooting, and he had a reputation for being particularly helpful to newcomers. He did have one firm rule: He stopped work at 5 p.m. Most companies keep shooting until 6 p.m. or after.

Pa didn't object to starting an hour earlier in the morning and he never complained about the number of scenes he did during the day. But when 5 p.m. arrived, he had just one interest—getting home in time to spend the early evening hours with the children and me. Clark always made this point clear to producers before starting a picture, so there was never any trouble. The crew used to joke that he'd be off the set at two minutes after five. Often, he didn't even stop to remove his makeup before hopping into his little sports car and heading out over the freeway to Encino. If there was one thing Clark loved after his family and his home, it was that car.

The children looked forward to Pa's homecoming each evening as much as he did. When they were smaller, Bunker and Joan used to take their little play chairs out to the edge of the driveway and sit waiting for him. They would be alerted by the red light which flashes whenever the electric gate opens, and Clark barely had a chance to climb out of the car before they were all over him. He'd hoist Bunker up on top of his shoulders and Joan would hang on piggy-back and this is how the three of them would arrive in the house.

LOOK MAGAZINE PHOTO

Bunker grimaces as Joan gives him a sisterly kiss at the ranch in 1956, about one year after our marriage. The affection and love their stepfather and I had for each other seems to have been contagious. The children adored Clark and often addressed him as "Dearest Stepfather."

DICK FISKE

Report card day. Clark is reviewing Joan and Bunker's reports, and delivering a lecture about how important summer reading is, and how important education is throughout life.

As the children grew older, this routine varied somewhat. When Bunker started attending a military school way across town, he sometimes didn't get home until after Clark. (When Bunks first put on his little uniform, Pa affectionately dubbed him "General.") The boy would come in through the kitchen and stop to check on what we were having for dinner. Then he'd hear Pa's voice in the living room and he'd come dashing in to greet him. He'd tear across the room, hit the back of Pa's favorite chair, make a leap for his shoulders and end up balancing on top of them.

I remember one particular afternoon when Bunks really smacked against the chair in executing his running leap. He perched happily up on Clark's shoulders and inquired, "Pa, what happened at the studio today? Did you kiss Marilyn Monroe?"

"No, General," Clark answered good-naturedly, "I didn't kiss Marilyn Monroe." Then his voice grew stern as he added, "Now Bunker, I have told you 50, maybe 100 times, I want you to stop running through the dining room and hitting the back of this chair. You're breaking it down."

There was a brief pause, then Bunker jumped to the floor. He leaned on the arm of the chair and looked directly into Clark's eyes. (We had carefully taught the children that when they talked to someone, they should look right at them.) So Bunks gave Clark his straightest look and seriously inquired, "Pa, what do you want, broken furniture or a warped personality?"

Somehow, Clark managed to keep a straight face. We certainly chuckled over it later, and the next day he got a big kick out of repeating the story on the set.

Our evenings were always pleasant and the routine much the same, even when Clark wasn't working. It always amused and pleased me that he looked for me the minute he came in the house. He'd hardly be through the doorway before he'd sing out "Ma!" Sometimes, when I had been to the market, I'd leave my car outside the kitchen entrance. When he didn't see it in the garage, he'd immediately call, "Louise, where's Mrs. Gable?"

I made it a point to have everything in order. In cool weather, Clark would find an inviting fire burning in the living room and in warm

LOOK MAGAZINE PHOTO

Bunker, like his stepfather, is an avid reader.

weather the electric fans would be blowing a refreshing breeze. And always there was a background of soft music from the hi-fi.

I made sure I was presentable, too. My husband never found me still wearing pin-curls or lounging around in a housecoat. At least, not if I could help it. I always tried to allow myself the time to bathe and freshen up before Pa arrived home. I've never been one to spend hours primping. Frankly, fooling around with a lot of make-up bores me. The few times I've tried to get fancy with it, I've succeeded only in proving I'm not the type. Instead of tracing an exotic line around my eye, I'd usually score a bull's-eye with the pencil. So I've never bothered with these time-consuming details, but I have always taken pride in being neat, clean and well-groomed. Clark admired this in a woman.

If it had been an extremely warm day or if I knew Clark had been working on a dusty, hot set, I'd try to wear something that would be pleasing and cool for him to look at. I'd select a white linen dress or a fresh blouse and skirt. Pa always noticed what I was wearing and if he didn't like a certain outfit, he'd diplomatically let me know.

We both looked forward to that pleasant time before dinner. After greeting the children, Clark would relax in his favorite chair. Actually, he had four favorite chairs; the big overstuffed one in the living room, the leather one in his upstairs study, another overstuffed one in the

Bunker's 10th birthday party at our rented Villa St. Antonio in Albana, Italy. I had a hectic time trying to find the cowboy decor in Rome. Bunker's guest on the left is Marietto Angeletti who appeared with Clark in *It Started In Naples*.

WIDE WORLD

library and the big, comfortable bamboo chair on the screened porch. I usually had a cocktail ready for us; Pa liked a little vodka mixed with fresh grapefruit juice. There was another little ritual we used to enjoy. Clark would light two cigarettes and gallantly place one in my mouth.

The children usually ate earlier than we did, but often we'd sit with them while they had their meal. Sometimes we'd all gather in the den and the children would eat at the little old-fashioned school desks I'd picked up in an antique shop. Clark and I would have dinner at 7 p.m., but we seldom ate in the large dining room. Sometimes we'd have our meal at the cozy little table in the breakfast area off the dining room. Often we'd have it on trays in the library, in front of the living room fireplace, upstairs in our bedroom or out on the porch. We'd eat anywhere we felt like—it all depended on the weather and our mood.

Our meals were usually quite simple but I always made sure they were attractively served. We'd have steak or chops or some roast meat and a green salad. Dessert was generally fresh grapefruit; right off our own trees, I might add.

Clark was never fussy about food. He liked it prepared simply. Rich sauces and fancy concoctions were not his cup of tea, which incidentally was the beverage he preferred. However, Pa was insistent about one thing—he wanted meals served right on schedule. Lunch should be ready at noontime, not 1:30 or 2 p.m. And dinner was always served at 7 p.m. I suppose, as with most men, Clark's favorite dish was a good steak. And you could always tempt him with potato salad, salami and kosher dill pickles. We both considered a big plate of sauerkraut and knockwurst one of the finer things in life, followed closely by sauerbraten and potato pancakes and Pennsylvania Dutch cole slaw. Pa used to boast I made the best Pennsylvania Dutch cole slaw in the world and naturally, I never tried to convince him otherwise.

There was one other delicacy of which Clark was mighty fond, but he diplomatically restricted his indulgence to the times when we were out hunting or fishing. He'd cut thick slices off a big white onion and sandwich them between slices of the homemade bread I'd always remember to bring along. A dinner at Maxim's couldn't have pleased him more.

A victorious day for our son. Bunker and Pa left for the duck club early o
Thanksgiving morning and returned with their bag lim
and very ready for dinne

LOOK MAGAZINE PHO

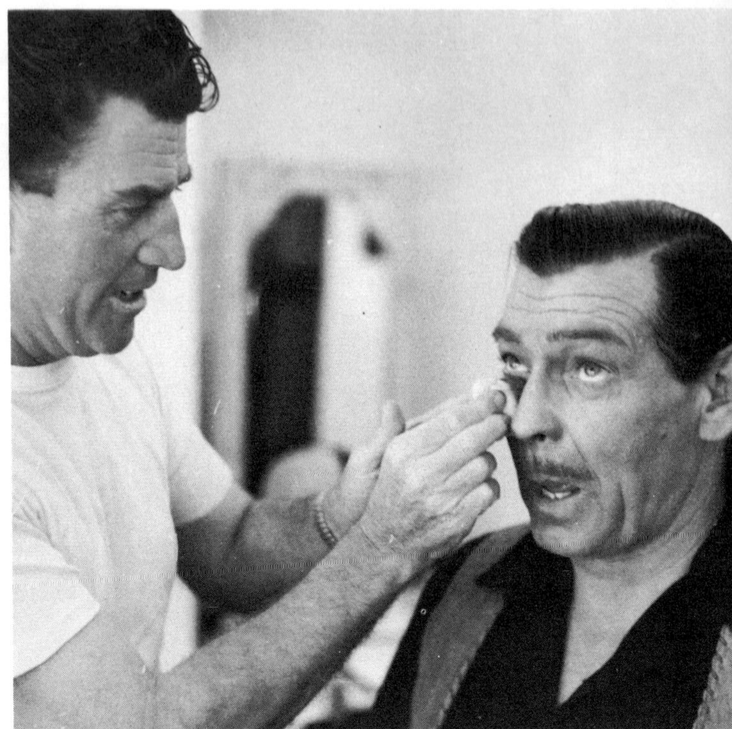

LOOK MAGAZINE PHOTO

(Left) Clark wore very little make-up when making a movie. Once I tried to make him darken his slightly gray mustache with an eyebrow pencil. I did not succeed. (Right) Make-up artist Don Roberson—with Mr. G.

Perhaps it was the influence of our early farm days, but both Clark and I preferred going to bed early and getting up early. Of course, when Pa was working, an early curfew was a necessity, but even when he wasn't, our lights were generally out by 9 or 10 p.m. We used to joke that on some evenings we'd be in bed before the children. However, either one or both of us would be sure to listen to their bedtime prayers each night.

After dinner we'd read or just sit and chat and sometimes we'd watch television. We had a big color set in our bedroom, a wedding gift from Pa's dear friend and agent, George Chasin. Frankly, Clark was never a great TV fan. But he was an enthusiastic sports fan, so if a sporting event was being televised, we'd tune in. Clark liked to catch the Wednesday and Friday night boxing matches and he never missed the football and baseball games and the golf and tennis matches. He knew a lot about these sports. The only one he wasn't particularly interested in was horse racing.

Pa thought Red Skelton was one of the greatest comedians and he generally watched his show. Though he'd received fabulous offers, he steadfastly refused to make any TV appearances himself, with the exception of one Academy Awards program in which he participated. Clark was intensely loyal to the medium which had made him a star and there was no offer large enough to sway him from movies to television.

Motion picture business requires many people, who seldom receive public recognition—but are vitally important to the actor and the industry . . . I requested this personally autographed photograph of Clark's efficient crew—most of them worked hand in glove with their boss for 25 years. Upper left, make-up artist Frank Prehoda; Mr. G's stand-in Bob Davis; Clark's wardrobe manager Swede Munden; "Poor Pa" as he autographed this, and Lew Smith, dialogue director. Lew doubled for Clark years ago in many pictures.

Sometimes, as an after-dinner treat for the children, we'd have a little corn-popping session in the library. I'd preside over the electric popper and I'll have to admit it was just as much of a treat for us. Clark loved popcorn. He also loved jelly beans and old-fashioned hard candies. I used to put them in quaint old apothecary jars which were placed strategically about the house. There was always a good supply in the bedroom along with a big bowl of fresh fruit.

When we were first married, Clark had a glassed-in gun cabinet running the length of one wall in the library. He took great pride in his gun collection, which included a number of antique arms and dueling pistols. I particularly remember a neat row of gleaming hunting knives. Clark felt all this might prove too tempting to my inquisitive youngsters. "I don't think it's a good idea to have guns in view of little children," he said. Even though he dearly loved that cabinet, he promptly called in a carpenter to rip it out and replace it with bookshelves. The collection was locked away out of sight and never once did Clark voice the slightest regret or complaint. But I noticed a sad little smile on his face as he watched the remodeling work.

It didn't take long for those new shelves to become heavy with books; the shelves in his upstairs study were already overflowing. Clark was one of the most avid readers I've ever known. He averaged a book a day and his taste ranged from Thurber to Thoreau. He had a complete, and well-thumbed, set of Shakespeare and he relished biographies, histories and books on current events. I remember he particularly enjoyed the Churchill memoirs. Pa always read the morning and evening papers and we subscribed to several of the weekly and monthly magazines. His favorites were *The New Yorker, Harper's* and *The Atlantic.*

Clark had one of those wonderful big Webster's unabridged dictionaries on a stand in his study and he frequently made use of it. "I enjoy learning more about words," he once remarked. He also encouraged Bunker in a do-it-yourself semantics course. One day Bunks asked Clark what a certain word meant. "Why don't you go look it up in my dictionary?" Pa replied. "Oh, that's too much trouble, and besides, I'm not sure how to do it," the boy said.

FPG

(left) Clark, in our garden, enjoying his favorite pastime, reading. The book is by Clay Fisher, who wrote *The Tall Men.*

(below) Scripts were one thing that Clark always received in abundance. Many writers turned out screen plays with him in mind, hopeful that he'd say yes and play the part, which they had written for him. Wherever we went the scripts followed us. Of course he couldn't do them all, but he did try to read everything submitted to him, and he was always kind and courteous in his refusal. In this picture I have a book I'd like him to read, but it looks like I'll have to stand in line.

LOOK MAGAZINE PHOTO

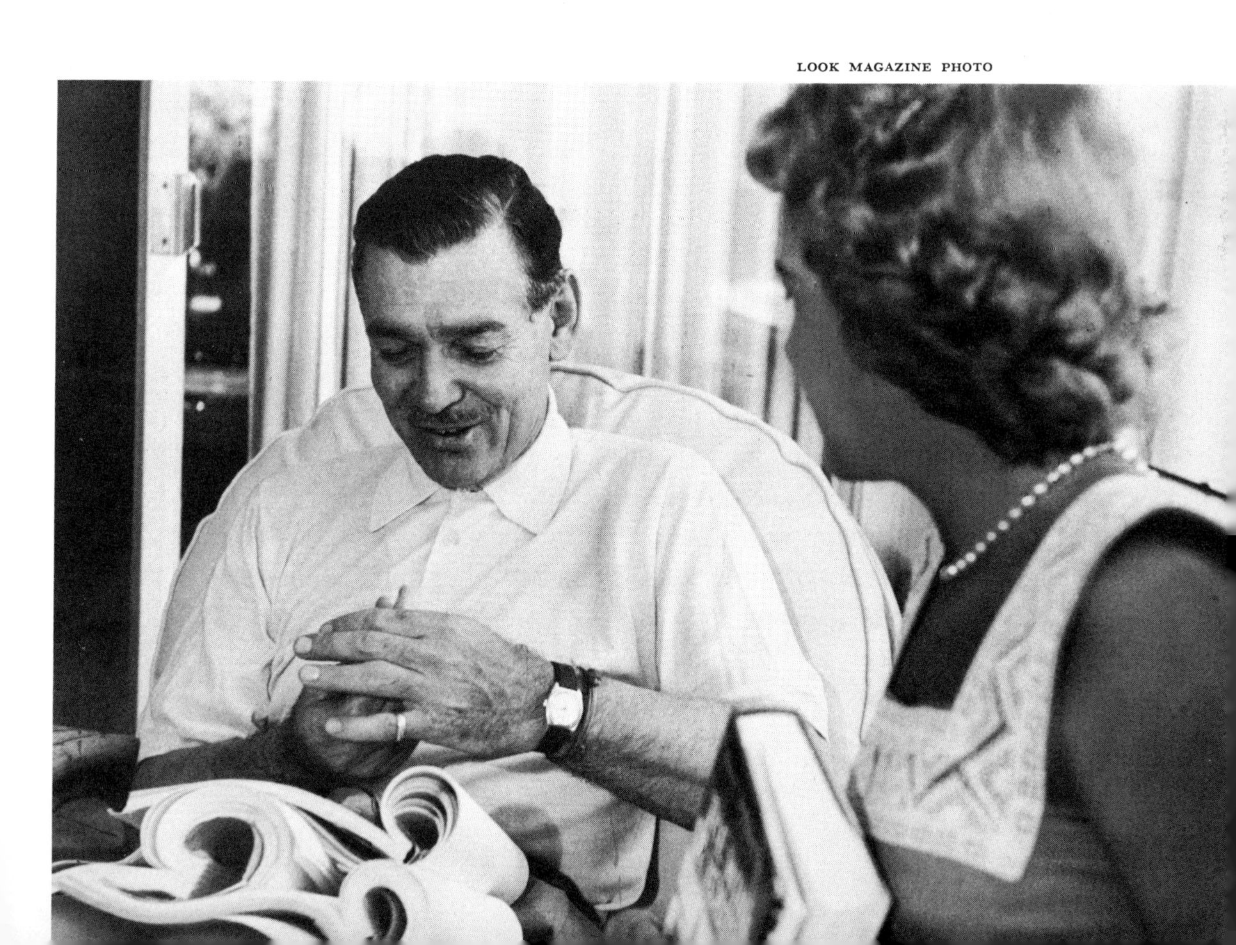

LOOK MAGAZINE PHOTO

Pa here is enjoying the snows of Sun Valley during a skiing trip, and is waiting for Earl Theisen to snap this photo so that he can extricate his leg from the deep drifts.

Clark's voice was friendly, but firm. "No, son, you must never say it's too much trouble to learn something. Come on, let's go look that word up in the dictionary. I'll show you how—it's really a lot of fun."

Pa was proud of both the children and he used to boast to friends: "Their mother's done a wonderful job with them—she's responsible for their good manners." But I knew Clark's love and intelligent handling deserved much of the credit. While he and Bunker had quickly developed a warm man-to-man relationship, Pa was equally close to Joan. In fact, I often thought he understood her and handled her better than I did. She'd come bouncing into our bedroom in the mornings with a

My favorite hunter—as usual, he's bagged his lim

LOOK MAGAZINE PHOTO

LOOK MAGAZINE P

(left) This was Clark's lucky fishing hat. It was hard to get it away from him, but when anyone did, they always caught a fish. Pa loved that old, beat-up chapeau. (right) Clark stretches and exults and just plain glories in the joy of living after a long battle with a marlin.

special greeting for Pa. "Good morning, dearest Stepfather," she'd say, then she'd plant a big kiss on his cheek and skip out of the room. At the door she always paused and flashed him her most flirtatious smile. It pleased and amused him.

There was one point Clark always tried to make clear to the children. As their step-father, he loved them very much, but they were never to forget that they had their own father, too. Clark never attempted to steal love away from anyone.

When he wasn't working, Pa spent considerable time with the youngsters. Since they lived on a ranch, Clark suggested they might like to join the 4-H Club. Their first project was raising a lamb, and Clark, a farm boy and animal lover at heart, practically made it *his* project.

Swimming was another favorite pastime, and the three of them spent many hours in the pool. Joan had quickly adopted one of Clark's pet expressions and after every few strokes she'd call out, "How'm I doing?" Clark also taught both youngsters to ride and under his expert instruction Bunker also soon learned to handle a rod and a gun.

One day Pa outfitted the entire family with racing bicycles and this led to numerous Sunday outings. We'd pack a big picnic lunch and pedal for miles out in the San Fernando Valley. Sometimes we'd put the bikes in the station wagon and drive some distance until we found roads that had little traffic.

Joan and Bunker loved our family fishing trips. One summer we spent a week in a little log cabin on the Mackenzie River in Oregon. Clark was a wonderful fly fisherman and he liked to use a very light rod. So I bought him a present of a one-ounce rod and he rewarded us all by catching trout after trout. Clark taught us how to clean the fish, shake them in a paper sack of cornmeal, then fry them. He also showed us the best way to eat them—just pick those delicious crisp little fish up in your hands and polish them off like an ear of corn. We usually accounted for five or six apiece, and while we may have dined in fancier style, I doubt we ever had a fish dinner that tasted so good.

Clark took a great interest in helping me plan the children's future education. One night when we were discussing the merits of certain prep schools and colleges, Joan asked Pa what college he'd attended. "The college of hard knocks," he told her with a smile. "What kind of school is that?" Bunker spoke up. Clark gave him an affectionate look. "You'll find out some day," he said.

A few days later Joan came home from school and marched up to Pa, who sat reading in one of his favorite chairs. "Dearest Stepfather," she began. "I asked our teacher and she said there is no such school as the college of hard knocks."

Clark put down his book, squinted and raised his eyebrows in that characteristic way of his. But his smile was warm as he took Joan's hand and replied, "I don't like to contradict your teacher, Joan, but I'm afraid some day you'll find out there is."

Neither of the children was aware of Clark's fame as an actor. They

LOOK MAGAZINE PHOTO

My favorite fisherman takes time out for a long smoke during an angling holiday at La Paz, Mexico.

knew he made movies, but they attached no more importance to this than if he had gone to work at a bank or office building. Pa never talked about himself as a star. So they could never quite understand why he attracted so much attention when they were out together. One year Bunker asked Clark to take him to the Halloween festivities at a nearby public park. Pa hesitated, remembering what had happened the year before when he had accompanied the children. He was quickly recognized and surrounded by autograph seekers the rest of the evening. Not only did he personally shy from such attention, Clark also felt all the commotion was unfair to the children.

This time Bunker had it all figured out. He had been to the dime store where they were selling rubber masks fashioned in the likenesses of various movie stars. "Here, Pa, I've got a perfect Halloween disguise for you," Bunker explained as he proudly presented Clark with a paper sack. "You can go to the park with us and nobody will ever recognize you—just wear this Clark Gable mask."

The best part of this story was the discovery Clark made when he laughingly agreed to try on the "disguise." In his excitement over his big idea, Bunker had picked up the first mask he found with a mustache. "Holy Smoke!" Clark roared as he pulled the rubber mask over his face, "you've turned me into Walter Pidgeon!"

When Bunker joined the Encino Little League, Clark not only gave him moral support, he spent many an afternoon practicing with him.

Chocolate cake was another of Clark's favorite foods, but only while not working on a picture. He bites into a healthy mouthful of the home-made variety during a breathing spell on one of his fishing trips.

LOOK MAGAZINE PHOTO

LOOK MAGAZINE PHOTO

Just pure, plain, raw onion was another favorite. Pa loved to just slice 'em and eat 'em.

The two of them would get so interested in throwing "hot grounders," I'd often have to go out after them three times before they'd finally come in for dinner.

After Clark died, Bunker would come home from school, pick up his baseball and go out to the paddock all by himself. He'd throw the ball, then run like a deer to catch it. Sometimes he'd do this for hours and I'd watch from the window, sharing his loneliness. One late afternoon he came in, wearily tossed his ball and mitt on the chair and said, "Mother, I miss Pa so much."

"Yes," I said, "we all do—the whole world does." Bunker fiddled with his mitt for a moment, then added, "But I miss him for so many special things. If he were only here to throw me some hot grounders."

Clark's delight in Bunker and Joan served to increase his desire for a third child in the family. It was indeed a happy day when, two months after we were married, the doctor told me I was pregnant. I hurried home to Clark; this was the most wonderful news I could ever bring him. Pa was overwhelmed. He was so pleased he just sat there beaming. This was what he wanted more than anything in the world. He was going to be a father for the first time—and here he was 55.

That big, happy smile didn't leave his face for days. In fact, it was the smile which gave our secret away after we'd decided not to tell anyone about the baby until I was a little further along. We attended a dinner party where someone remarked, "Clark, that's an exceptionally big grin you've been wearing all evening. Has someone just given you a private key to Fort Knox?" The big grin grew even bigger. "Better than that," Pa blurted out. "Next May I'm going to be passing out cigars." That did it. The next day anybody who could read a newspaper knew the Gables were expecting.

During the tenth week of my pregnancy I contracted a virus which I couldn't shake. I ran a high temperature and was given strong medication which left me quite weak. Shortly after this I had a relapse and suffered terrible pains. Clark called the doctor and an ambulance and we went to the hospital. At 4 a.m. the doctor said, "I'm sorry; I've done everything possible, but I can't save your baby." He ordered me to surgery.

When I regained consciousness, I was dimly aware of Pa standing beside me. My eyes filled with tears—I had so wanted to give him a child of his own. I noticed Clark's hands, gripping the side rails of my hospital bed and when I looked up I could see he was biting his lower lip hard in an attempt to control his emotions. Neither of us said anything for a moment. There was no need to put into words what the loss of the baby meant. Each knew how the other felt. Finally, Clark managed a weak smile. "There, there, darling, don't worry," he consoled me. "We'll have our baby yet."

Clark's comforting prediction didn't come true for almost six years, but they were busy and happy years for us. We celebrated birthdays, holidays, built a desert home, went hunting and fishing and made our first trip to New York together. And, of course, Pa continued to work hard. He made several pictures and I always accompanied him on location, as did the children whenever they were out of school.

Looking back, I particularly remember our first Thanksgiving together. We had invited my family for dinner. My brother Vince was there with his attractive wife, Marie, and three of their children. My sister Elizabeth, the wittiest, prettiest blonde I know, was on hand with her good-looking husband, Gordon, and their young daughter. Bunker and Joan rounded out our cheerful, hungry group. Of course I'm prejudiced, but I remember thinking what a charming family picture they made. The living room looked particularly cozy that day with its old pine, cherry and maple furniture, the knotty pine walls rubbed with white paint, the hunting prints, the plump, quilted sofas and chairs in pleasant greens, pale yellows and an occasional touch of soft red. The old coal-oil lamps were burning, reflecting on the red roses I had picked that morning and arranged in antique pewter mugs.

Yes, it was a warm, happy scene that Clark surveyed when we gathered around the long pine table in the dining room. He was seated at one end and I at the other. The huge turkey made its appearance, invoking a chorus of admiring "ohs" and "ahs." My eyes met Pa's and we exchanged smiles. Suddenly, he pushed back his chair, walked the

I love Clark's expression—one I often see on John Clark's face—without cigarette, of course! My husband taught me to roll my own. I'm fair at On the left is Jack Butler, who lives in a tent year-round in the Ka National Forest. Thirty years ago Clark would hunt mountain lions w him for weeks. Jack taught Mr. G. to make a bough bed to sleep in a hours of hunting. Clark would never kill a deer, but never hesitated shoot mountain lions because they prey on d

LOOK MAGAZINE PH

(right) This is a tiring way to teach your wife to shoot, throwing clay birds, using a hand trap. We did this on Pa's Sundays off at the Utah location. Nothing was ever too much for Clark, if it brought good results.

LOOK MAGAZINE PHOTO

(below) Ready for some jump shooting at Kulican, Mexico. My teacher was very pleased that morning. I shot 27 ducks. The guide said I was the best woman shot he had ever seen on the lake. I asked him how many women had shot there. "You're the first one," he admitted.

length of the table and kissed me—right in front of everybody. "Kathleen," he said softly, "thank you for giving me my first real Thanksgiving."

We always looked forward to Christmas at the ranch. Clark had acquired two strings of old reindeer bells and we always hung these on red ribbons on either side of the dining room entrance. Fresh English holly spiraled up the staircase. Pa had some definite theories about Christmas decorations—they should be just red and green and traditionally old-fashioned. He disliked the modern glittering pink, white, purple, and blue trees and always selected the biggest natural green one on the lot. Usually, we'd have to chop off a bit to get it in the room.

Clark's method of trimming the tree I'm sure will sound familiar to many wives. He'd go through the elaborate motions of hanging a grand total of three ornaments, then retire to the safe distance of a comfortable chair, from which he would frequently issue directions to the rest of us. But if anybody asked later, why, certainly he helped decorate that beautiful tree!

One thing Clark never tired of was hunting. One day, shortly after we were married, he asked me if I'd like to learn to shoot. "I'd like to try," I answered. And so began my education. My teacher was thorough and had infinite patience, which I matched with earnest determination. Clark taught me what he later taught Bunker—that a gun is not a toy, but a weapon to be kept in perfect order, to be handled with respect and to be fired only under certain circumstances.

Pa started me out with a 20-gauge Remington shotgun. He made me carry that gun unloaded for one whole year in the field, until he was satisfied I could handle it safely. Clark's shooting lessons were augmented with training from the pro at our skeet club in Chatsworth. It was a big day when I bagged my first bird. Pa was as proud as I was. "I'm making a fine hunter out of you," he announced. "A huntress," I corrected him.

Clark was a crack shot and he kept our freezer well-stocked with pheasant. He'd save the pretty tail feathers for the children to make Indian headbands. In time, I became a fairly good shot and my husband was already ready to compliment me. I felt I had graduated with honors the day he presented me with a beautiful new Winchester.

CLARK and I didn't spend all our time in the duck blinds. In November of 1958 we flew to New York to see some shows, do some special Christmas shopping and visit a number of friends. New York is always an exciting city and this was the first time we had ever been there together, which made it more so. In contrast to our quiet life in Encino, we were having quite a fling. Our schedule was a busy one, what with our shopping sessions, the theater and numerous dinner and party invitations.

One afternoon Pa popped me into a cab and announced, "I'm taking you to Cartier's. I want to buy you something nice." Clark ushered me into the famous store. With great ceremony, Jules Glaenzer himself showed us stone after stone. Finally, I turned to Clark, who was finding the building's steam heat as uncomfortable as I was.

"Pa, it's so warm in here," I said. "What I'd really like is to go over to Abercrombie's and get fitted for that new gun." So off we went, leaving Mr. Glaenzer with the most bewildered expression he'd worn in years. As he smilingly told me later, "I never thought I'd see the day when a woman would turn down our jewelry in favor of a rifle."

I have always prided myself on being well organized, so naturally I was in charge of our busy schedule in New York. Clark depended on me to get us to the right party or theater at the right time. One night we had tickets for *Bells Are Ringing.* As we dressed, I reminded Clark we were scheduled to stop by the home of our friends, Mr. and Mrs. T. (Tommy) Suffern Tailer, for a little snack before the theater, so we wouldn't have to bother with dinner, I pointed out.

There was a terrible blizzard that night, but luckily we had a car and driver. We arrived at the Tailer's apartment and rang the bell. Tommy himself answered the door. He was in his shirt sleeves with hair tousled and I caught a glimpse of a woman flying down the hall in a housecoat and curlers. There was no mistaking the look on Tommy's face when he saw us. He registered complete surprise.

When our devoted maid, Louise Washington Jones, was married at The Church of the Divine Guidance in Los Angeles, the boss and I attended. Pa gave the bride away. The church was packed. I was touched by the warm reception the congregation gave my husband.

LOOK MAGAZINE PHOTO

Jane Russell and her leading man, going over a scene from *The Tall Men,* in Durango, Mexico. The script book you see in Clark's hand was one he used for 25 years, it was made by a friend of his who did beautiful leather work.

"Oh," I faltered, "are we early?" Tommy's surprise gave way to laughter. "Only by a week," he grinned. I didn't dare look at my husband.

It turned out the Tailer's servants were off and they themselves were dressing to go to a party. But they insisted we at least come in for a drink. By the time we left, Clark had been fortified by cocktails but no before-theatre snack. Checking my wristwatch, I realized there wasn't time to grab even a sandwich before the 8:30 curtain. And to make matters worse, we'd had an early and very light lunch.

So we hurried to the theater. While Pa checked his coat, I bought some chocolate bars in the lobby. Influenced by hunger and a sweet tooth, I selected $1.25 worth. When I opened my purse to pay, I discovered I'd forgotten to bring any money. I explained to the girl I'd have to wait for my husband to come and bail me out. By this time, everyone in the lobby had recognized Clark, including the cute little candy clerk, who was craning her neck to get a better look at him. When he walked up to pay for my chocolate, she all but fainted. "Is *Clark Gable* your husband?" she sighed, "Oh, I'm so glad you didn't have any money with you."

Finally we reached our seats, only to be told after we had made ourselves comfortable that we were in the wrong row. After some commotion, we found the right seats. Then Clark remembered he'd left his good hat under the other one. But at this point he was in no mood to go back for it.

As the lights dimmed I started to peel the wrapping from a candy bar. Perhaps it was just the hushed theater, but never have I heard cellophane make such a loud, crackling noise. The woman in front of me looked around indignantly. Chagrined, I waited for the covering sound of the opening applause, then yanked frantically at the offending wrapper. I offered Clark some candy. He shoved it aside. "I don't want to eat any chocolate," he said, his voice louder than necessary. The woman in front swiveled around again. I felt like a character in a Sid Caesar sketch.

About five minutes later, Clark's head began to droop. I nudged him gently. He ignored me. The combination of the steam-heated theater, the cocktails and what turned out to be the beginning of a bad cold, was just too much for him—he was sound asleep. Then, just as it was deadly quiet on stage, Clark snored loudly. I nudged him, this time not so gently. Simultaneously, the woman seated on his other side gave him the elbow. Clark's head shot up and he emitted a loud and surprised grunt. Once more we received a reproving look from our neighbor in front.

At last the first act was over. I suggested leaving, but Pa felt it would be impolite to the actors. During intermission we hurried across the street to Sardi's. I figured a sandwich would improve the situation. But Clark stubbornly said no. He gave me the look of a man who had just conceived a brilliant idea. "I'm going to have a drink," he announced.

When we got back to the theater almost every one else was seated, and the lights were dimming as we started down the aisle. Suddenly they went bright again and there was a tremendous burst of applause. It took me a moment to realize it was for my husband. As we walked to our seats the entire audience stood and applauded. It was a spontaneous ovation and it brought proud tears to my eyes. I squeezed Pa's hand. He smiled at me and teased, "You should have come to New York with me before. Now you know what people think of your old man."

After the show, Clark said, "Let's go to the '21' and have some dinner." I suggested we go to the Stork Club instead, explaining I'd like to see Sherman Billingsley. At this time the club was caught in the middle of a labor dispute between two unions. Clark hesitated. "I don't like to go through a picket line," he said. But I begged him to do it for Sherman and finally he relented.

We walked in and glanced around—we were the only two people in the room! Clark looked at me. He didn't say a word—he didn't have to. His expression said it all. I had fixed up his evening just fine.

Clark's hunger overcame his annoyance and we sat down and ordered a big dinner—steak, baked potatoes, fried onion rings and green salad with Roquefort dressing. Sherman hurried up to greet us, followed by a procession of waiters bearing gifts. Sherm is famous for giving expensive favors to his customers. Our small table was crowded with

LOOK MAGAZINE PHOTO

No matter what outfit my husband wore, he looked right—even with a beard and a parka. This photo was taken during the shooting of *Across The Wide Missouri*.

Clark in fur-trader's garb for *Across The Wide Missouri.*

LOOK MAGAZINE PHOTO

A friendly horse looks on as Pa studies a script on location.

LOOK MAGAZINE PHOTO

bottles of perfume, champagne and other items. Pa looked it all over, his mood definitely not improving.

I thought to myself, "Well, things can't get any worse." But I was wrong. Just as the platoon of waiters started serving our food, a party of eight noisy people came in and seated themselves across from us. That is, seven of them sat down. The eighth, a large woman with a loud, raucous voice, weaved over to our table crying, "My God, Clark Gable! I've been in love with you all my life." Then, ignoring me completely, she proceeded to tell Clark her life story. It must have been a hilarious scene. There we sat, trapped at the tiny table, completely surrounded by this woman, about 14 waiters and our untouched dinners.

We looked at each other. "Mrs. Gable," Pa said in a slightly formal tone. "I have lost my appetite. Let's go."

So that was our big night on the town. When we got back to the hotel we laughed about it. I said to Clark, "Wasn't that a delightful evening? Don't you think I handle our engagements beautifully?" Pa returned my smile. "Yes, Kathleen," he said. "You're really a very clever girl. You fixed us up just dandy."

Whether we were at home or away, Clark was always as concerned about my health and comfort as I was about his. When I became ill with what was diagnosed as a heart condition in 1956, he spent every minute he could with me. He even moved into the hospital during my six-week stay. Later, when the doctor ordered me to spend seven months in bed recuperating, Clark was a most devoted nurse. He wouldn't even let me reach for a book. And he watched over me like a hawk, making sure I followed all the doctor's instructions.

Even after my illness was almost over, he kept checking up on me, making sure I got plenty of rest. His concern for my health led to an amusing incident when we were on location in Baton Rouge, Louisiana, where Clark was filming *Band of Angels.* The governor's wife had invited me to join her and the wives of other officials on a tour of some of the fine old ante-bellum mansions. I had not been feeling well and the long tour proved quite tiring. I had to take several nitro-glycerin pills during the course of the afternoon.

We were late getting back to the hotel and I knew Clark would have returned from the set and would be worrying about me. My hostesses were anxious to meet him and I invited them in, figuring that at least their presence would delay any scolding. But I figured wrong. Clark briefly, though politely, acknowledged the introductions. Then, while the surprised Southern ladies looked on, he turned to me. His voice was stern. "My, Kathleen, you're a nice gray color. You know I don't like you staying out so long when you're not well. You're going to

When Clark returned from the war and starred with Greer Garson in *Adventure,* the slogan around Hollywood was: "Gable's back and Garson's got him."

MGM

MGM

Pa played an advertising man in *The Hucksters* (1947). Sydney Greenstreet played his boss.

MGM

Command Decision had a star-studded cast. Left to right are: John Hodiak, Walter Pidgeon, Van Johnson, Charles Bickford and Clark.

bed this minute. I'll have some dinner sent in for you." Our visitors hurried their departure and I meekly headed for bed.

Then I remembered that our maid, Louise, who usually accompanied us on location, had complained that her room was uncomfortably cold in the mornings. So I located the little electric heater we'd brought along and took it to her adjoining room. I was just handing it to her when she suddenly froze, her eyes widening in surprise at something she saw behind me. At the same moment someone kicked me—right in my most kickable spot. I turned, and there stood Clark, in his bare feet.

"I told you to get into bed," he growled. "What are you doing in here, fussing around with a heater?"

"Why, you kicked me!" I cried, with all the injured dignity I could summon. "How could you do such a thing? You've never done anything like that to me before."

"Next time I'll have my boot on," Clark replied, with just the suggestion of a grin. "You know the doctor told you to take it easy. Now you get back in bed this minute." And with that, he kissed me gently on the forehead and brought me a tray with a light supper.

My husband was a genuinely modest man. In all the time we were together I can honestly say I never once detected the slightest sign of an over-developed ego. Pa seldom talked about himself and he never boasted about his screen success, his looks or the effect he was supposed to have on women. These things simply didn't occur to Gable, the man. As Gable, the actor, he was always conscientious and professional. Of course he was aware of his fame and he deeply appreciated the loyalty and support he'd received from fans for so many years. He felt an obligation to them and to the industry always to do his best, but he had no exaggerated sense of self-importance.

A close friend once asked me how Clark really felt about being labeled "The King." My answer was that he simply never mentioned it. I can't recall the subject ever being discussed. In fact, I don't think he ever thought about it. In the beginning, I imagine the extravagance of the title must have embarrassed him. However, I do recall that Clark became extremely annoyed when friends would laughingly recount

MGM

In *Mogambo,* Ava Gardner, Grace Kelly (now Princess Grace of Monaco) and their leading man.

stories about women visitors swooning over him at the studio. I quickly learned not to tease him about such things.

Clark was an honest man, both with himself and with others. In return, he expected people to be truthful with him. He liked directness in those he worked with and he'd really lecture the children if he caught them telling fibs. They never managed to fool him—he always insisted they look straight at him when they spoke to him. Pa used to say he never trusted a man who wouldn't look him in the eye when he talked to him.

One of the qualities I admired most in my husband was his understanding and tolerance. Clark simply had no religious prejudices. He never asked nor cared what church his friends attended. He never judged a person as a Catholic, Jew or Protestant. Nor was he biased in any way about race or color. It didn't matter to him whether a person was Nordic, Semitic, Latin or Oriental. What did matter was that his friends be decent human beings. If Clark thought someone despicable, he'd have nothing more to do with him. But he didn't make a big fuss about it; he simply dismissed the person from his mind.

I never heard Clark make an unfavorable remark about someone's personal characteristics, race or religion. And he always quickly stopped others who did—in a tactful, but firm manner. I think Arthur Miller said it best in his dedication of his book, *The Misfits*. "To Clark Gable, who did not know how to hate." I will treasure that line always, because I know so well how true it is.

Clark and I were so happy about our expected heir that we used to spend hours planning his nursery and talking about his future. By the time I was five months along, we had even got as far as discussing colleges. One day, shortly before Clark's fatal illness, I brought up the subject of religion. "Pa, what about the baby's religion?" I asked. I knew Clark had been baptized a Catholic, his mother's faith. His father was a Methodist. I thought he might have some preference.

Clark didn't answer my question for several minutes. Then he said, "Well, Kathleen, you were baptized a Catholic and you're bringing up Joan and Bunker the same way. You know more about your religion than I do. So, let's baptize the baby a Catholic. I know you'd like that."

He paused a moment, then continued: "Religion is so personal a matter." We smiled at each other and that settled it.

My husband was always a complete gentleman, in private as well as in public. I don't think he ever did or said anything out of line, unless you want to count that friendly little kick in Baton Rouge. I recall

An informal shot of Sophia Loren and Clark at Ana Capri, Italy—a location used for the filming of *It Started In Naples*

WIDE WORLD

Arthur Miller's remark about Pa: "Of all the actors I've known, Clark Gable was the only real man I ever met—the finest and truest gentleman."

Though he was always polite, Clark was never stuffy. He had a wonderful sense of humor. He was always ready to laugh, even if the joke was on him. Pa used to roar at some of the corny jokes I'd recite during our long hunting trips. He never cared much for vulgar or "sick" jokes. He liked his humor clean. And he always got a big boot out of the funny things the children would say.

Clark is shown deeply at work (work?) between scenes of *The King and Four Queens* in Utah. Left to right are actresses Barbara Nichols, Eleanor Parker, Sara Shane, and Jean Willes.

I fixed Pa's breakfast every morning while on the *King and Four Queens* location in Utah. I also sent him to work with a home-made lunch. The clock on the wall says 6:45 A.M. Who says a movie star's life is easy!

LOOK MAGAZINE PHOTO

LOOK MAGAZINE PHOTO

My friendly Mormon neighbors at St. George, Utah used to invite me to afternoon quilting sessions while Pa was busy on the set.

It has been reported that Clark loved practical jokes. This was definitely not true, at least not during the years I knew him. Clark hated them. However, one night I pulled a little surprise on him which he thoroughly enjoyed.

I told him we were invited to a big, black-tie party at the home of a famous star, and that I felt we really should attend. He didn't jump with joy, but he agreed to go. On the appointed night we dressed and came downstairs together. Clark looked wonderful in his soft white dress shirt and his well-cut jacket. He never went in for a lot of jewelry: he liked beautiful wrist watches, but he refused to wear ornate shirt studs or large, fancy cuff links. His taste ran to simple accessories of good quality.

Pa nodded approval of my short black chiffon gown and for a few minutes we stood there at the foot of the stairs, our mutual-admiration society in session. I suggested before leaving that we have a glass of champagne in honor of our rare evening out. As he put down his glass, Clark made his usual before-party remark. "I hate having to get dressed in dinner clothes and I'm not particularly mad about going to this thing —so, old gal, let's be on our way and get it over with."

I stalled, suggesting another glass of wine. Punctual Pa looked at his watch and headed for the door. "You said we were to be there at 8 p.m. and that's just when we're getting there. I'll go get the car out."

After a few minutes I sent Martin out with the explanation that I wasn't quite ready and wanted Pa to come back in the house. I could hear Clark grumbling before he even reached the door. When he walked in, he found the dining room doors open, the coal-oil lamps aglow and the table beautifully set for two. And waiting to be eaten was his favorite dinner of knockwurst, sauerkraut and boiled potatoes.

"I fooled you, Pa," I smiled. "This is the party you're invited to." Clark's surprised expression gave way to a pleased grin. "Ma, I'm so glad you asked me," he said. He kissed me on the cheek. "I love you," he added. "Now let's eat."

On the rare occasions when we did go to big dinner parties, we never stayed late. Along about 10 or 11 o'clock I'd get a wink from Pa, the signal for me to be ready to leave soon. I never kept him waiting; we'd thank our host and hostess and head home. Then, still in our evening clothes, we'd go up to his study and observe a little ritual. We'd open a bottle of champagne and toast each other. We'd sit and talk, and sometimes laugh, until about 4 o'clock in the morning. These were private and precious hours and I will never forget them.

Clark was essentially a conservative man. He never made snap judgments or decisions and he disliked ostentation. It has been said he was overly thrifty. This wasn't quite true. To be sure, Clark was cautious and careful about investments, his contracts and other business matters. What man with common sense isn't? Clark had the best lawyers and agents and he intelligently followed their expert advice. Pa was not a silly spendthrift, but neither was he stingy. He was, in fact, quite generous with his family, his friends, his employees and co-workers. If there was anything I needed or wanted, he never counted the cost.

Clark always insisted on paying his own way; he never tried to work angles or get things free. Though he was often approached to endorse products, he always refused. We could have had a new electric kitchen, a new pool or the house refurnished several times over, but Clark wouldn't play it that way. "I always like to pay for what I get," he'd say.

Pa didn't care a fig about status-symbols. Of course, to some degree, stardom and financial success affected his way of life—but not his outlook on life. His hobbies, his tastes, his basic standards and principles would have been the same if he had never been a big star. Clark was not a show-off, nor was he the type for luxurious self-indulgence. But there was one thing for which he had a great weakness—he was crazy about beautiful, fast sports cars. From the time he was a very young man he'd had a great enthusiasm for driving fast cars, racing motorcycles and tinkering with engines. Pa had a mechanic's appreciation for the precision engineering that went into a car like his sleek Mercedes 300 SL. And he had a typical man's attitude about allowing a mere woman to drive it. I was never even permitted to pull an ash tray out of that car.

It amused me that Clark hesitated so long before buying it. We already had a big Mercedes sedan as a family car and Pa felt he was being duly extravagant in hankering after the sports model. He debated with himself for weeks. He'd take it out on test runs, lovingly examine the motor, then come home and fret about it. Finally, I said, "Pa, why don't you get that car? You're so crazy about. I don't think it's a silly extravagance. After all, you seldom buy anything for yourself and you've worked so hard. You have the money—go get it. All I ask is that you keep the speedometer under 100."

So Clark acquired a new love and he took care of that car as if it were the Kohinoor diamond. One day when I was riding with him, he

ABBIE ROWE

Clark and I were so proud of this picture with President Eisenhower. It was taken in 1958 when we were in Washington for the opening of Pa's film *Teacher's Pet.* While we were lunching in the Senate dining-room, it was suggested that we take a quick look at the White House. We had no appointment with the President, and had not asked for one. A senator ushered us into the Cabinet room and to our surprise and delight President Eisenhower came out of his office. He offered Clark his hand and said warmly "From one public servant to another—how are you Major Gable?" Clark had met the General during the war. During our pleasant chat Clark and Ike talked golf. The President cheerfully remarked that he was going to baby-sit with his grandchildren that evening so that his son and wife (John and Barbara Eisenhower) could attend the preview of Pa's picture. Mr. Eisenhower then called an aide and instructed him to show us the projection room which he and Mrs. Eisenhower used frequently. "Also show Mrs. Gable the china room—she may enjoy looking at the china patterns of the past First Ladies," he added. Then he grinned and said, "Oh, well, show them everything." I shall never forget that visit or the President's warmth and graciousness. It was my first visit to the White House although Clark had been there before with Carole for a fireside chat with F. D. R.

The reason for the radiant glow on our faces here at the premiere of *The Tall Men* in 1955 was that I was expecting. One month later we were grief stricken over the loss of our little one.

made the supreme, unselfish gesture—he offered to let me drive. "Let's see if you have the proper touch for it," he said, as I took the wheel. Nervous in the presence of the great master, I pulled away from the curb. I shifted into what seemed like 16 different gears, wrestling the lever all the way. The accelerator definitely preferred a size 12 brogan to my daintier slipper. The car and I fought it out for a block, then Clark sadly rendered his verdict.

"Move over, Ma," he said, shaking his head. "I love you, but you just don't have the touch. You're not driving this car."

Another car, of much earlier vintage, highlighted the celebration of our fifth wedding anniversary in 1960. Clark and I revisited the scene of our elopement, retracing every step. We even arranged a sentimental reunion with Julie and Al Menasco under the same grove of cottonwood trees. Before meeting our friends, we stopped to freshen up at the same motel where we had dressed for our wedding. We were given the same room Pa had used that day. We changed clothes, iced the champagne we'd brought along to toast the occasion and started out for our rendezvous with the Menascos. As Pa was backing the gleaming Mercedes out the driveway, he spotted a 1914 Model T Ford in the motel owner's garage.

"I'll give you $25 if you let me drive it just to meet our friends," Clark propositioned him. The owner was delighted to oblige. It was a blistering hot day and Clark had some difficulty getting the car started. Finally we sputtered off at 15 miles an hour with our champagne. Our arrival was a howling success.

"When does the honeymoon end?" said Al, shaking his head in amused wonder.

"Never," I answered quickly. "With us—never."

Though Clark was always well-dressed and certainly had an adequate wardrobe, he didn't spend an excessive amount of time or money at the tailor's. He preferred casual clothes and he had some favorite old sport coats from which he refused to be parted. Clark always took such good care of his things, they seemed to last forever. Once he sent me to the closet to get a suit he was particularly fond of. I called back, "Do you mean this gray one with the 1802 label?"

"I didn't ask for comedy, Kathleen, just bring the suit," Clark retorted. But he laughed, too.

There was a little cedar-lined room off Pa's study which I referred to as his "hope chest." It was here that he kept all his sports gear, his old boots, sweaters, jackets and the khaki shirts and trousers he wore hunting and fishing and when working around the ranch. How Clark loved those khaki outfits! On him they looked as if they'd been tailored on Saville Row. No matter what he put on, Clark always looked just right and at ease, whether it was a pair of levis and cowboy shirt or white tie and tails. This wasn't a studied or even conscious effort on Clark's part—he simply had innate grace and style. But he had something more—more than just his fine physique, good looks and superb coordination. He had an air of virility, vitality and authority, and it was as natural to Clark as breathing. Perhaps this is what some of the writers meant when they referred to his "magnetic appeal." Whatever it was Clark had, it brightened any room he entered. It also brightened my life.

Clark's distinctive appearance made him easily recognized in public. But what continually amazed me was the way people could spot him from a great distance. No matter what he was wearing or doing, after only a fast glimpse, they knew it was Pa. I remember we'd go horseback riding on the bridle paths near the highway in Palm Springs. Cars driving past at 50 and 60 miles an hour would suddenly skid to a stop and friendly strangers would call out, "How are you, Clark? You're one of my favorite actors."

But the strangest occurrence of this kind was in 1959 when we were in the Austrian Alps. We were helping the children build a snowman and Clark was all bundled up in a heavy coat and scarf and wore a Tyrolean hat with a feather sticking up. Some men who were repairing the road passed by. They glanced our way, then began yelling, "*Clock Gobble, Clock Gobble!*" On that far-off mountain peak or in deepest Africa—wherever my husband went, people knew him and loved him.

I remember one occasion when I pulled a funny switch on Pa. We were at the airport in Trinidad. I stopped at a souvenir stand to buy a book for the children. I couldn't resist the title—*Mother Goose Rhymes*

Along with the rest of the world, Ingrid Bergman, who held Gary Coop
and Clark in great esteem, has a heavy heart over their passing—within
few months of each other. A gay ski trip at Sun Valley for them in 194

U

UNITED ARTISTS

The Misfits, Clark and Marilyn, in a love scene.

in Calypso. When I looked for Clark, he was surrounded by a group of women eagerly seeking his autograph. I edged my way through the crowd. Pa was busily signing right and left. When I reached his side, I shoved my Mother Goose book at him. He promptly autographed it and handed it back. Then he did a double-take and grinned. "Please, Kathleen," he said, "not so early in the morning."

The year after Pa and I were married we built a house adjoining the golf course at Bermuda Dunes, outside of Palm Springs. When we first discussed the project, Clark was somewhat dubious; he wasn't sure he'd want to spend much time there. As it turned out, he was crazy about the place. We both loved the house and the life we led there. In fact, we became such confirmed "desert mice," we'd stay on long after the season was over and most other residents had fled the heat.

Clark had great respect for the author of *The Misfits,* Arthur Miller, whom you see going over pictures with Clark. After Clark's death, Arthur came to our ranch and gave me a copy of the book version of *Misfits,* dedicated "To Clark Gable, who did not know how to hate," and with an inscription to me: "Dear Kay, may this help us all endure, remembering the power of his goodness and his love. With my gratitude to you. Arthur. January 5, 1961."

UNITED ARTISTS

The house itself could never be called pretentious but we thought it very attractive and comfortable. We planned it in simple contemporary style, with an eye to maximum comfort and minimum care. Clark never liked having a large staff of servants around and we rarely had any help at all in the desert house. I did the cooking and cleaning. Pa did all the marketing and also served as official observer at dishwashing time. To be fair about it, I relegated to him the role of onlooker. Clark often offered to help, but I've always felt that dishwashing was a job a wife should be able to handle herself.

However, I did put Clark to work hulling strawberries. On his first attempt, he attacked the berries with a knife. I quickly showed him how to remove the little green stems neatly with a spoon, the way my mother had taught me. From then on, he was chief strawberry huller and I used to joke that he was the fastest spoon in the West.

Director John Huston and the star discussing the next scene for *The Misfits.*

UNITED ARTISTS

UNITED ARTISTS

On the *Misfits* location we have a "cast family portrait" around the ladder. Shown here are Frank Taylor, the producer, writer Arthur Miller, director John Huston, the fine actor Eli Wallach, Montgomery Clift, Marilyn Monroe and the King.

EVE ARNOLD, MAGNUM

A very dramatic shot of Marilyn Monroe with her leading man from the final scene of *The Misfits*. Clark told me the director was having trouble with the dog seen in this picture. The director wanted to use our hunting dog and pay him $500.00 per week. Mr. G. said no, one actor in the family was enough.

One year, when we stayed on the desert from January to June, Clark played golf every day. Each night I'd fix a tray with grapefruit and tea or coffee all ready for Clark to plug in when he got up at 5:30 or 6 a.m. Then he'd go out and practice his putting. About 8 o'clock he'd be back in, calling out, "Say, old lady, I'm a little hungry. How about some bacon and eggs?" I'd be ready for him. "Yes sir, coming right up," I'd cheerfully promise.

Then we'd enjoy a leisurely breakfast, sitting tailor fashion on the white vinyl floor in the living room, our plates on the low coffee table. Clark had helped me plan the decor of the house. We used off-whites and beiges throughout the entire house, with a few touches of lacquer red as an accent color. I'd always try to have a bouquet of fresh red carnations in the living room. The effect was one of uncluttered coolness.

Some days, Clark would play golf with his Bermuda Dunes buddies. "I've got a little game on today with the boys," he'd announce, his tone a little apologetic. "That's all right with me," I'd assure him. "I've got a little match scheduled with the ironing board." So Pa would kiss me and hurry off and I'd do my ironing by the big window in the living room, which faced the 6th fairway.

But before starting, I'd fill a big pitcher with cold water, add eight teabags and set it out in the hot desert sun. I'd leave it there, steeping

Clark with Montgomery Clift roping the wild mustangs. My heart would ache when Pa would return home in the evening from the *Misfits* location all covered with dust, throat sore, and exhausted. Why he didn't use his double for this rugged work, I don't know. I do know I yelled my head off because he didn't. After his shower we would have an early dinner, two aspirins, and I would do the honors with the liniment.

UNITED ARTISTS

and heating in the sunshine, until Clark and his friends came by. Then I'd bring out ice cubes and we'd all have a glass of the best iced tea ever brewed. I learned this method from a friend years ago; it makes the most wonderful tea I've ever tasted. But the trick is to have a temperature of at least 110 degrees in the sun.

My husband also loved lemonade and I used to fill an old-fashioned brown jug with it and put it in his electric golf cart. That cart was the last birthday present I ever gave him. I will never forget his delighted surprise when he first saw it. It was charcoal grey with a white fringed awning on top and I had a big C.G. painted on the side. Clark loved the cart, but he was a little embarrassed by the monogram. "It's kind of corny to go riding around with your initials all over the place," he protested.

"Well, if I want to be a little corny once in a while, please let me," I pleaded. Pa laughed and the corn stayed.

Clark found the desert both revitalizing and relaxing. He was bronzed, trim and fit when we all left for the Reno location of *The Misfits* in July of 1960. Admiring my tanned, handsome husband in his cowboy shirt and snug-fitting jeans that first day of shooting, I had not the slightest hint that these were to be the last five months of his life.

It is painful for me to recall the frustrations and tensions Pa endured during those rugged months of filming. But it is of great comfort for me to remember that it was also during this period he received word of what he joyously called "the greatest blessing of my life." For it was while we were in Reno we learned I was pregnant. At last, after one bitter disappointment and years of hoping, Clark was to have a child of his own.

I will never forget the afternoon we got the results of the laboratory tests. It was August 7, my 43rd birthday and Clark had accompanied me to the office of a Reno doctor. "Mrs. Gable," the physician said, smiling down at the report on his desk, "you have yourself a wonderful birthday present—you are pregnant; the baby will arrive sometime next March."

Hand in hand, Pa and I left the office and returned to the home we had rented just outside Reno. I never saw a man so jubilant, so grateful.

…a watches as our friend Ernie Dunlevie tries a long putt at Bermuda Dunes.

…HN D. ROCHE

GAYLE'S STUDIO

On Clark's 59th birthday, I surprised him with this golf cart. The gift was a smashing success.

"My God, Kathleen," he kept repeating. "It's a miracle—a miracle. I can't believe it. At last, we're going to have a baby in the house. It will be like starting all over again."

It was such a happy afternoon. We started planning for the baby right then—you'd have thought it was expected the following week. At one point, Pa grinned and said, "Kathleen, you're 43 and I'm 59. Why, just think, between us we're 102 years old and here we are having a baby!" We both roared over that one. In fact, we laughed at anything and everything that lovely day. We were so sure Clark was right. We were starting all over again and we had a life-long lease on true contentment.

Pa and I kept the news a secret until my doctor assured us all danger of another miscarriage was past. Once the word was out, reporters hurried to the *Misfits* set to confirm it. Clark, who in the past had always been reticent with the press about personal matters, happily told them it was true.

"Yes," he beamed, "Kathleen and I are expecting a child. Isn't it something—at my age? I consider this a precious dividend that has come to me late in life."

Of course, almost everyone asked Pa whether he wanted a boy or a girl. He always answered he had no preference; he just wanted a baby. But secretly, I prayed for a boy, because I knew what a son would mean to Clark.

Joan and Bunker eagerly anticipated the blessed event. Joan was positive I was going to have a girl, but Bunker kept insisting he had ordered a little brother. The two of them would have vigorous discussions. Clark never took sides, but one night he turned to me and said, "Kathleen, a few months after this baby is born, I hope you'll become pregnant again. So if we have a girl for Joan this time, we can have a boy for Bunker next time." Smiling, I agreed—with all my heart.

While Pa was delighted about his impending fatherhood, he was far from happy with the slow progress on *The Misfits*. Characteristically, he kept his feelings to himself. Not once did he complain, either on the set or at home. Nor did he ever criticize anyone for the many

delays and the endless hours he spent waiting on the set. Considering the mental and physical pressures he was under, I marvel that he never once blew up on the set. It was a masterful exhibition of self-control.

Most of the film was shot on a blistering hot dry lake bed 50 miles from Reno. The thermometer generally registered 100 degrees early in the day and soared to a miserable 135 degrees by mid-afternoon. The alkali dust blew until it was scarcely possible to breathe. Many members of the cast and crew became ill. But Clark's physical stamina seemed indestructible; he outrode and outwalked men half his age. He did take after strenuous take where he roped a wild stallion single-handed.

Clark enjoyed hard work, but his own punctuality made it difficult for him to tolerate tardiness. He was the first one to arrive on the set each morning. A disciplined professional, he was already to work, always knew his lines. Naturally, it was frustrating for him to spend hours waiting. He'd come home at night, covered with that thick alkali dust and exhausted by the heat, the tensions and the eternal waiting.

One evening when he was showering after work, I heard Pa yell and I dashed in to see what was wrong. "It's nothing," he hurriedly assured me. But I discovered raw brush burns on one whole side of his body. Clark explained they had filmed a scene in which he was dragged on a rope behind a truck going 30 miles an hour.

I was appalled. "Why are you doing those scenes?" I asked. "You've got an expert stunt man who's supposed to do them." Then Clark hesitantly confessed that he'd found the sitting and waiting so demoralizing he'd volunteered to do the scenes just to keep occupied. "Well, you just stop it," I ordered with wifely authority. I put a cool compress on Clark's side and rubbed his back until he was relaxed enough to fall asleep.

The Misfits filming ran long past its scheduled finishing date, but at last it was over. Pa saw a rough version of most of the film in the studio projection room. He wanted me to go with him but I decided to wait and see the finished picture. Pa phoned me right after the screening to tell me how pleased he was. "I like it, Ma," he said. "I think it's the best thing I've done since *Gone With The Wind*.

t Bermuda Dunes Country Club near Palm Springs. The golfer is shown ith his friends Ray Ryan and Ernie Dunlevie.

YLE'S STUDIO

HARRY LA CHANCE

The cool, comfortable living room at our Desert home.

The last day Clark spent in the house he loved began much as any other day on the ranch, except that it was raining. It was Saturday, Nov. 5, 1960. The night before, Pa had finally finished all work on *The*

Misfits and he came home looking so worn out my heart ached for him. He talked of flying up to the duck club near Stockton for the weekend, but changed his mind.

Saturday morning he looked more rested. We had breakfast. Then later in the day Pa took his hunting dog out to one of our back fields and worked him. He was pleased with the dog's performance and we talked about future hunting trips. Pa played with Joan and Bunker for awhile, then he seemed quite tired and restless—so unlike him. So I said, "Come on Pa, you had better get a good night's rest, so off to bed."

About 4 a.m. Clark awakened with a bad headache. I gave him some aspirin and he dozed fitfully. There was a terrific thunder and lightning storm—a rare occurrence in California—and it vaguely disturbed me. I was concerned about Pa and it was some time before I went back to sleep. At 8 a.m., I woke to find Clark standing in the doorway. He had started to put on a pair of his favorite khakis but he had been unable to finish dressing. His face was grey and beaded with perspiration.

"Ma, I have a terrible pain," he said. "It must be indigestion." I was frightened by his appearance but I tried to keep my voice calm as I helped him to a chair. "I'm calling a doctor," I said. "No, don't," Pa protested. "This will go away in a while. I don't need a doctor." I looked at Clark sitting there helplessly, then I reached for the phone. As I dialed I said, "I've never disobeyed you, Pa. But this time I'm sorry, you must have a doctor."

When the doctor arrived, he took one look at Clark and immediately put in a call for an ambulance and a fire department rescue unit. "Is it a coronary?" I whispered. The doctor said he thought it was.

It was so like Clark to be more concerned about me than himself, even though he was in great pain. He protested my riding in the ambulance with him; he was afraid it might prove too upsetting in my condition. Of course, I insisted on staying right beside him. As the attendants wheeled him out, Pa looked up at me and said, "I feel terrible, Ma, doing this to you." I gave Pa a reassuring smile as the ambulance headed out our drive, past his beloved oleander trees.

BOB LANDRY

Clark and I discuss a script during our European trip

For the next ten days I rarely left Clark's bedside. At first, I slept on a little cot at the foot of his bed. But his small room soon became crowded with medical equipment and the two nurses we used on each shift, so the doctor thought it best I move to an adjoining room.

It was a great shock for me to see Clark in a hospital bed. He had always been so vital, so strong, so full of life. He was never ill and previous checkups had shown nothing wrong with his heart. Though he suffered great pain at the time of his attack, Clark never complained. He was a good patient and determined he'd get well. His main concern was for me and our baby. "Look what I'm doing to you and the baby," he kept fretting. "I shouldn't be keeping you cooped up here. It's the worst possible thing for you." I'd fix his pillows, then answer, "You're wrong, Pa. Being here with you is the *only* possible thing for me."

From the start, Clark insisted on knowing the truth about his condition. "I want to know just how bad it is," he told the heart specialist. "I want to know how much damage there's been and how active I can be in the future. Just give me the plain facts; don't varnish them. I can handle it." Pa's courage never deserted him.

Clark was told that once he was out of the hospital he would face a long period of rest. After that he could gradually resume his normal activities. Each day he seemed a little better; he even felt well enough to read five of the twenty books I'd brought him from Hunter's book store in Beverly Hills. I also brought in two little elbow pillows so he could read more comfortably. Clark looked at me over the top of his reading glasses. "Come on, old lady," he protested. "Let's not overdo this. I'm not quite that fragile." We both laughed, but I noticed he enjoyed the pillows all the same.

Pa continued to look forward to the baby. I was five months pregnant then, and he used to say, "Kathleen, stand by my bed sideways—I just want to look at you." One of my dearest and last memories of my husband was the look of proud anticipation on his face the day we borrowed the doctor's stethoscope and he listened to his son's heartbeat. "You must have Mr. America in there," he said. Today, when I hold John Clark in my arms, I remind myself that at least Pa had that much.

After Clark's attack, the doctors explained the tenth day was generally the crucial one for a coronary patient. I recall one of them say-

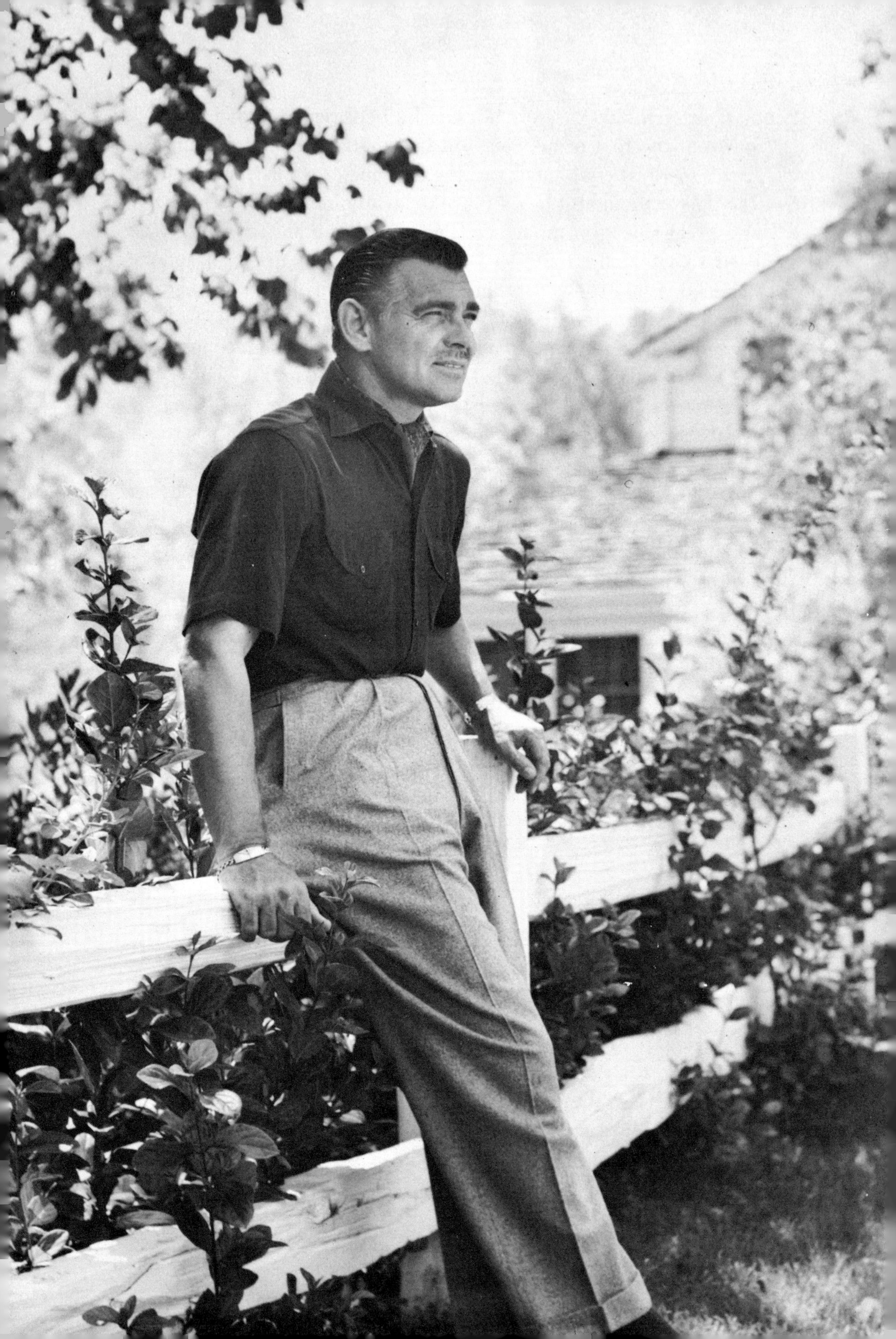

ing, "If we get through the tenth day, all is well." So I counted and I prayed. On the ninth day I went home to gather up some things for Pa. I had no premonition of Clark's death. There was no reason I should. He appeared to be doing so well. From that first frightening moment on Sunday morning I had faced the situation with prayers, not tears. I was determined to be strong for my husband and the child we expected. But as I moved about our bedroom that afternoon gathering up the items Clark had requested, I suddenly broke down. I locked myself in the bathroom and wept. Finally, I pulled myself together and, dry-eyed, hurried back to the hospital.

When I entered his room, Clark looked at me and said, "Oh, God, Ma, don't leave me again. I don't want to be alone."

The next day, Wednesday, November 16, we all felt encouraged. I brought in some of the letters and telegrams which had been arriving by the hundreds each day. Each afternoon I'd select a small number for Clark to read.

"Here's one from an old girl friend of yours in Paris," I said, handing him a sealed envelope. "See, I didn't even open it." Clark flashed me that characteristic grin. "Where are you hiding the rest?" he teased.

I sat next to Pa's bed, watching his reflection in the mirror. I had never seen him look so handsome, so serene, in all the years I had known him. It was almost miraculous, I thought. The marks of his illness—the lines, the strain and the pallor—were gone. Clark looked twenty years younger and his expression was strangely peaceful. I've heard it said the flame burns brightest just before it sputters out. But this never crossed my mind as I sat bathed in Clark's wonderful glow.

Later, Rufus Martin, our devoted houseman, who had been with Clark over twenty years, stopped in for a brief visit. He, too, was encouraged and left smiling. "I won't worry about Mr. Gable any more," he said.

Pa and I had a nice little dinner together and we commented on what a lovely day it had been. At 10 minutes past 10 p.m., I felt an angina attack coming on. I couldn't understand it; I hadn't had one for nearly two years. I didn't want Clark to worry, so I quickly made an excuse to leave the room. I kissed him and gave him a tender hug, saying, "Sweetheart, I'll be back after the nurses get you ready for the night. Then we'll drink our buttermilk together and I love you." They were the last words I spoke to my husband.

Over and over I have said to myself, "Oh, if I only hadn't left the room." But at least I know that it was over in a split second. The doctors assured me Clark suffered no pain—he didn't know he was dying. The nurse said he simply closed his eyes, his head fell back on the pillow and he was gone. It happened at 10:50 o'clock.

I had dozed off after going to my room and was awakened by the doctor and a nurse. "Clark has taken a turn for the worse," I thought I heard the doctor say. It was like a nightmare. The nurse seemed to be crying. I started to get up, then blacked out. In a few seconds I recovered. The doctor was rubbing my wrists. "What did you say?" I cried. This time I heard him clearly. "Clark has passed on."

"Let me go to him," I said, pushing myself up from the bed. "No," pleaded the doctor. "It's better for you to stay here." I reached for my robe. Nothing on this earth could have stopped me from going to Pa. I motioned the doctor and his sedatives aside and I went.

When I finally returned home, I went straight to Clark's study and sat in his favorite chair. I had refused any sedatives. I wanted my thinking clear; there was much I myself must do. This was not the time to collapse. I was determined not to let Pa and his baby down. I sat there a long time. It was early morning when I finally ordered some hot tea and sent for the children.

Calmly, but gently, I told Bunker and Joan that Clark was gone. They listened quietly, their faces white. They loved him so much. I put my arms around them. "I want you to remember Pa loved you both," I comforted. "One of the last things he did was to ask me to call home and find out how you were."

In death, Clark was accorded the dignity and respect he had always earned in life. I am so grateful that nothing marred the solemnity of the simple funeral services conducted at Forest Lawn Memorial Park. Clark had once remarked, after reading a distressing account of a famous star's last rites, "Please, Ma, don't ever let that happen to me. Don't let them make a circus out of it."

IRVING ANTLER

Louella Parsons wishes me luck with a kiss. My sister Elizabeth is on the right.

IRVING ANTLER

My dear friend, Mrs. Ray Hommes, gave a baby shower for me about three months before John Clark was born. Here you see (left to right) Miss Johanna Thomas, the children's governess; Mrs. Thayer Bigelow; my sister-in-law, Mrs. Vincent Williams; Mrs. Ernie Dunlevie, they are our neighbors across the fairway at Bermuda Dunes Country Club in Indio, California; Mrs. John Lee Mahin—John and Clark were in the 8th Air Force together. John wrote *Red Dust,* also the movie *Mogambo* for his favorite star. Joan and Bunker arrived from school to help carry John's many gifts home. Next Mrs. Hommes and another dear writer friend, Mrs. Kendis Rochlen Moss, and my sister.

IRVING ANTLER

Hedda Hopper also came to the baby shower to wish me luck. She gave John a little teething ring with a heart in the center.

In making the arrangements, I tried to carry out Clark's every wish. I buried my husband in his blue wedding suit and with his gold wedding band, his St. Jude medal, his last Christmas gift from Bunker and Joan. It was a terribly difficult day. I needed the memory of Clark's love and courage to get through it.

In the trying and lonely days that followed, one thought was uppermost in my mind—the birth of Clark's child. The loss of my husband was shattering and the tragedy that he would never hold his baby at times almost defeated me. But I was determined not to give in to grief. I owed it to Pa to carry on sensibly and calmly, making sure nothing went wrong in those last four months of my pregnancy. I am so grateful that nothing did.

I was not without help during this period. Bunker and Joan were a great comfort to me and, of course, they still are. But I have never believed in using children as a crutch, forcing them to share the weight of one's troubles. There were times when I was unable to hide my tears from them, but those occasions were few. And as Bunker would phrase it, I didn't ruin anything with my salt.

Clark and I had always encouraged intelligent questions from the children and we always tried to give them honest answers, never talking down to them. One afternoon, a few months after Clark died, Bunker found me in Pa's dressing room, sorting and packing away his clothes. It was a heart-rending task, particularly when I faced Clark's little "hope chest" room with all his favorite belongings.

"What are you doing?" Bunker wanted to know. I told him. He looked at me for a moment, then said, "You sure look sad."

"Well, Bunker," I explained, "it's a very sad thing when someone dies. They leave everything behind. Pa left all these things and now I must put them away."

Then Bunker explained something to me. "Don't you see, mother? It's really not sad. Pa doesn't need all these things now because he has many more precious things in heaven than he could ever have here."

One day I mentioned to the children that an old friend, a Jesuit priest, was coming to see me. I added that I was planning to return to

nding next to us after the christening is John Clark's godfather,
brother, Vincent Williams.

the Church after many years of non-attendance. Bunker's eyes went wide. "Wow, Mom!" he said. "When you go to confession, you're sure going to be in there a long time!"

My children's teasing aside, I have found solace and strength in my renewed belief. I do not look to my religion as a quick antidote for sorrow. Rather, I look to it for support and guidance on the difficult road to inner peace.

John Clark Gable was born in the same hospital where his father died 124 days before. I dreaded returning to that building and the sad memories it held for me, but there was a good reason why I did. My obstetrician, Dr. Richard N. Clark, who delivered Bunker and Joan, and in whom both Pa and I had great faith, was on the staff there. The birth was to be by Caesarean section and Dr. Clark explained he preferred operating with his own surgical team. Since I was anxious that nothing go wrong, I readily agreed. He, in turn, agreed to my request for a spinal, rather than a general, anesthetic. "I want to be conscious every minute," I said. "I want to be able to give the baby a big hug and kiss from Pa as soon as he's born."

As it turned out, I didn't get that kiss. They don't allow that sort of thing in surgery. But I did watch the birth in the reflection of the big light fixture above me. My first words when I saw my son were: "He's beautiful. Just what Pa wanted."

Later, when they brought the baby to me in my room, I struggled to keep my emotions under control. This was the moment which Clark had so eagerly anticipated. Here at last was his beautiful 8-pound son—the dividend he didn't live to enjoy. The nurses placed the child in my arms and tactfully left the room.

I examined my baby closely; he was absolutely perfect. Then I said his name out loud—John Clark Gable. It had been Pa's choice. He thought all three names sounded nice together. It is hard to put into words my feelings as I held our son that first day. How can you describe such a strange mixture of grief and gratitude, of unbearable sadness and great joy? I do know I felt that somehow Pa must be in that room with us.

As it was Clark's wish, John Clark was baptized a Roman Catholic. The ceremony took place at St. Cyril's Church in Encino, California on June 11, 1961. One hundred and fifty smiling guests were at the service. John Clark cried when Reverend Michael Lalor poured the Holy Water over his head. Now you see him leaving the church with his usual happy face. His exquisite christening gown was a gift from Don Loper. I, too, had a new gown made for this sacred occasion by my designer Werlé. Werlé thoughtfully made a burp cloth of the same material, to wear over my shoulder. Mrs. Jack Trent, John C.'s nurse is in the background holding J.C.'s robe and diapers.

One of my favorites—reminds me of a little bird in its nest.

LOOK MAGAZINE PHOTO

John Clark has brightened our home and the love that surrounds that dear little boy gives each day more meaning. His nursery is the happiest room in the house, and while Clark's presence is everywhere, I seem to feel it most in there. Pa helped plan the room, even to choosing the colors. The walls are a lovely butter yellow, the furniture is antique white and the cheerful orange and yellow floral print which we used on the window shades and the pillows was also Clark's selection.

I recall how pleased he was when we found a beautiful hand-carved maple four-poster baby bed made in 1852. We had it refinished in the antique white and it now boasts a white and yellow organdy-ruffled canopy. Often, as I stand beside that bed admiring its handsome little occupant, I am sure that my husband is standing there with me, his smile as proud as mine.

Every mother feels that her baby is the sweetest, the strongest, the smartest, the most beautiful and best-behaved baby in the whole world. I am no exception. John is all of that and then some. He looks exactly like his father. In fact, most of my friends refer to him as "Mr. Carbon Copy."

John's head is shaped exactly like Clark's. He has his facial features, the same long, straight legs and broad shoulders. His thick, dark hair—the first thing I noticed when he was born—combs naturally in the same style as his Pa's. In only one respect is John Clark unlike his father—he will never be teased about protruding ears.

But best of all, my little sweetheart even has his father's expressions. This is not just wishful thinking on my part—almost everyone who has visited him has noticed it. As early as his fourth week, John was raising one eyebrow and squinting at me in that characteristic way of Clark's. As Louise once commented, "Why, Mrs. Gable, that little boy is so much like his father, I feel as if it were Mr. Gable looking at us right now."

After John Clark's picture, taken when he was 14 days old, appeared on the cover of *Life,* I received thousands of letters which warmed my heart. Everyone agreed he did his father proud. I was both touched and cheered by the world-wide loving interest in our son. And I was amused by the comments in one particular letter. The writer wondered

John Clark loves to dance before his supper, so each evening at fiv
Joan, Bunker and I have a little dance with him. He leads ve
well. We call this "The Social Hou

LOOK MAGAZINE PHO

Cooing John Clark gives me an Eskimo kiss.

LOOK MAGAZINE PHOTO

John Clark after his tub, smiling from ear to ear.

LOOK MAGAZINE PHOTO

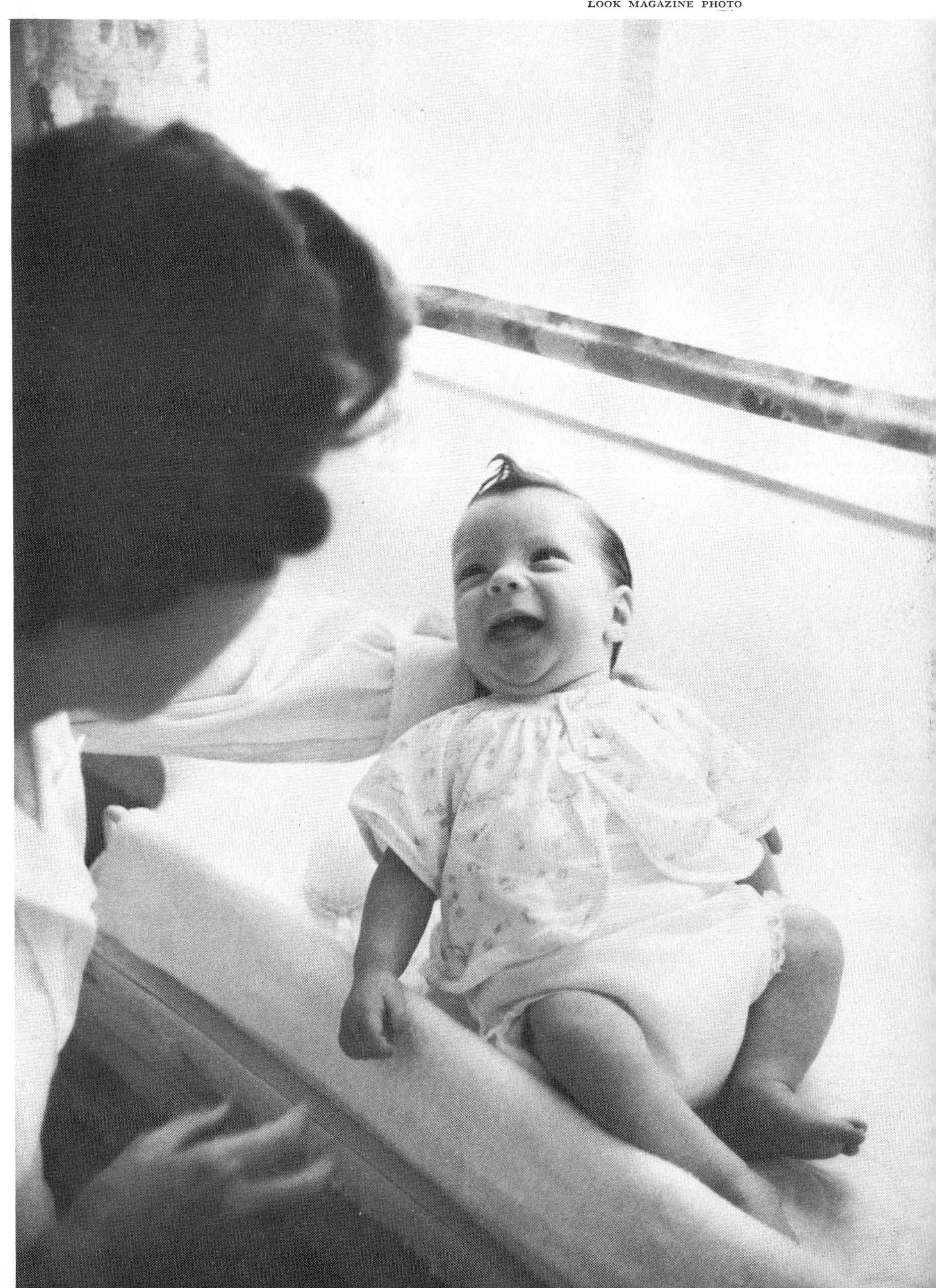

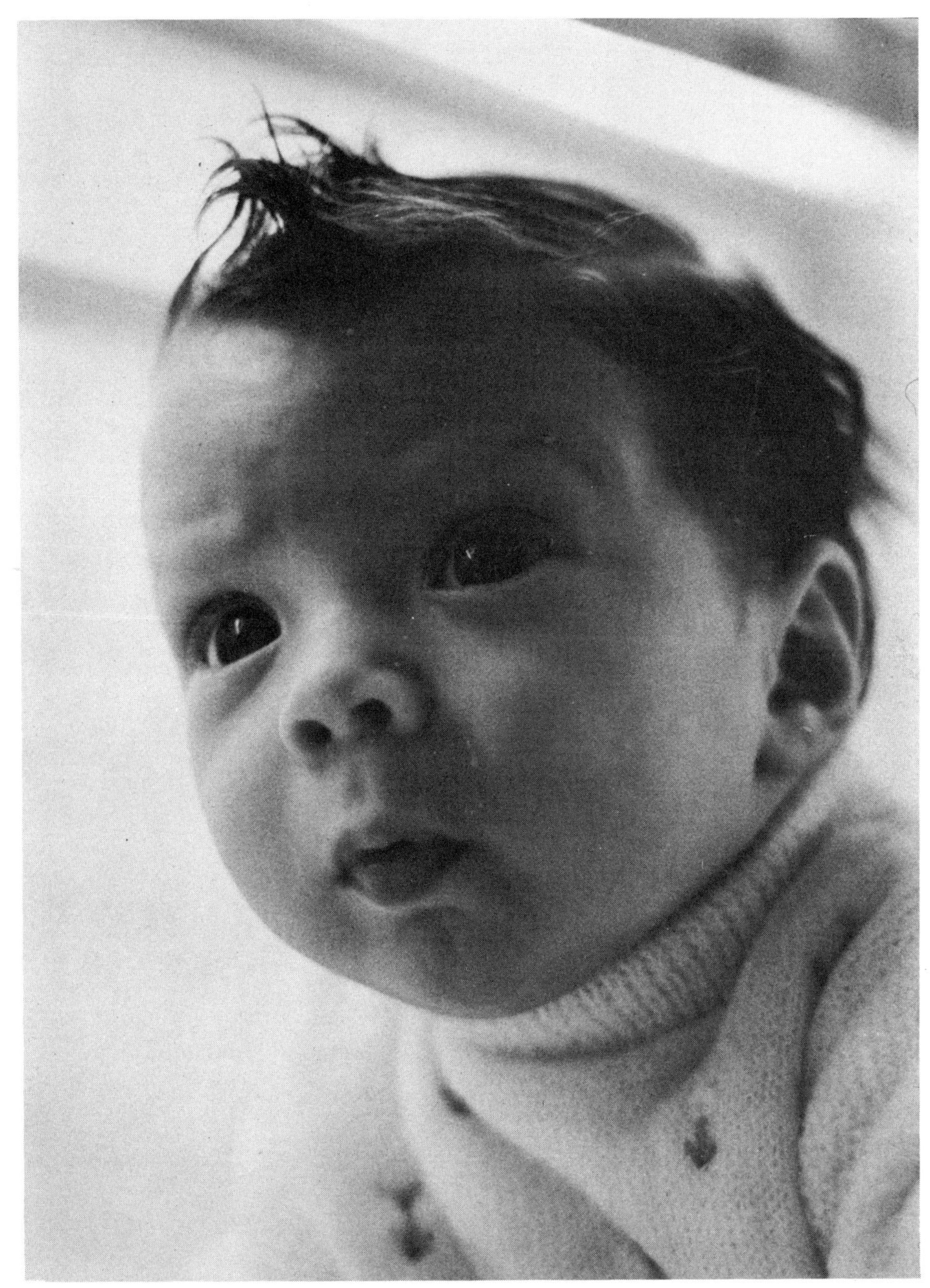

LOOK MAGAZINE PHOTO

John Clark's father made the turtleneck sweater famous. His son looks quite handsome in one.

ɔpposite) Nap time for little Gable.

OK MAGAZINE PHOTO

Clark Gable

if I hadn't hired Pa's make-up man to prepare John for his camera debut. "He's so handsome for a baby that age," the letter read, "and the resemblance to his father is so striking that it's hard to believe. He must have been wearing heavy makeup."

Joan and Bunker are as delighted with their brother as I am. Joan took one look at John and promptly forgot she ever wanted a sister. She is now my official assistant nurse, and I might add she is quite efficient. John loves having her sing little songs to him and she can change his diapers almost as fast as I can.

Bunker has big plans for his little brother. One day I came upon him in the nursery telling John all about it. "I'm going to get you a pair of blue jeans and a cool shirt and you'll be a real boy," Bunker promised. "And when you're big enough, I'll take you out to climb Pa's big tree with me."

On another occasion, when I let Bunker hold the baby during what we jokingly call his "social hour," Bunks looked down at him solemnly and said, "Man, you're O.K.—and you've got a real Daddy up in heaven who's looking out for you." That was one time when I refrained from correcting Bunker's cool slang.

When I first showed the children John's beautiful white lace christening dress and bonnet, Bunker was quick to protest. No brother of his was going to wear a sissie outfit like that, he announced. When I left the room, Bunks tried to hide the dress in the wastebasket. I rescued it and firmly straightened him out on the matter. "By the way," I added, as he left the room, "you should have seen yourself in yours."

Yes, children and love give life real meaning and each day I am so grateful for mine. Still, there are many bad hours, many days when I battle loneliness and despair, finding them the most formidable opponents.

I will always sorrow for Clark. But I will always find comfort in the remembrance of his love. And now I have his son. God blessed me very well.

here is a sad but precious story about the chair John Clark and I are sitng in. This was the canvas chair Clark used while on location in Nevada lming *The Misfits*. Bunker admired it one day when he visited his stepather on the location. On Christmas Eve I permit the children to open one ift from under the tree. On the Christmas Eve following Clark's death, unker chose a large crated box. In it was the chair he had admired.

OOK MAGAZINE PHOTO